Liz Cowell is a veteran family law specialist and arbitrator with more than 30 years' experience under her belt. Based in the North West of England, Liz has acted as partner at some of the region's most prestigious law firms and also works internationally with clients across the globe.

She sits regularly as Deputy District Judge, delivers training seminars to fellow family lawyers and most recently has launched a practice focusing on Arbitration, a form of Alternative Dispute Resolution recommended by the gridlocked family courts.

A regular contributor to the media both as writer and expert commentator, this is Liz's second book for Law Brief Publishing.

Married with two adult sons, Liz loves Cornwall (where she tries to spend any holiday time) and modern art. More details and her blog may be found at www.lcfamilylaw.co.uk.

The Journey to No Fault Divorce – A Practical Guide

The Journey to No Fault Divorce – A Practical Guide

Elizabeth Cowell LLB

Deputy District Judge

Family Law Arbitrator

Fellow of the International Academy of Family Lawyers

Solicitor, McAlister Family Law

Member of Resolution

Law Brief Publishing

Published 2022 by Law Brief Publishing, an imprint of Law Brief Publishing Ltd
30 The Parks
Minehead
Somerset
TA24 8BT

www.lawbriefpublishing.com

Paperback: 978-1-914608-55-1

To my father, Rod Cowell 1926 – 2021

Who encouraged and supported me on my journey to becoming a family lawyer

PREFACE

I saw the need to write this book, not only for my fellow family lawyers, but also for the general public, who could benefit from some clarity around divorce after two years of Covid-19, gridlocked family courts and most importantly a gamechanging new law.

Every so often, throughout history, there have been laws passed which have changed the way we regard marriage – and divorce. The Divorce Dissolution and Separation Act 2020 is one of them. This much-awaited Act became law in England and Wales on 6 April 2022, and changed the way couples get divorced. Previously, whereas one party could lay blame with the other, the new Act removed all the blame and the need for it – hence No Fault Divorce – enabling couples to end their marriage without having to blame or find fault with the other. Now, there was only one fact for divorce: irretrievable breakdown.

Moreover, divorce could now be done online – I explain all this in my book, and enclose the necessary form for practical purposes. I also thought it would be interesting to delve into the history which would eventually result in this new law, albeit a whistlestop tour, featuring a few of the many campaigners who helped pave the way to where we are today.

I would like to thank a few people for their encouragement, guidance – and work. Firstly: my late father, Rod Cowell who encouraged and supported me in my journey to becoming a family law specialist; my husband Lawrence for – as always - his unwavering support; my two sons, Emile and Joel who make me proud and whose chosen careers are somewhat similar to our own (we must have done something right!); and last, but not least, Raine Marcus who offered advice, copy and language editing skills throughout.

The law described in this book is believed to be correct as at 4th July 2022.

I hope you find *The Journey to No Fault Divorce – A Practical Guide* both useful and interesting.

Liz Cowell
July 2022

CONTENTS

CHAPTER ONE

INTRODUCTION

For millennia, sexual relationships between men and women have been governed by the religious authorities in most civilisations.

Throughout history women have been regarded as chattels: initially owned by their fathers, (and in some instances by their brothers) and then by their husbands. These relationships were controlled by the relevant theological bodies across the globe.

Same sex couples were rarely tolerated, and still aren't in many countries. Such couples were often persecuted with no protection in law. In fact, they are still persecuted today in many jurisdictions worldwide. In this jurisdiction – ie, in England and Wales – same sex couples can either marry or enter into a civil partnership. This has been achieved since relationships between adult male homosexuals were legalized following the Sexual Offences Act 1967.

Of the Abrahamic religions, both Judaism and Islam have always made provision for the breakdown of marriage, and have long established means of ending such unions. Furthermore, both religions allow for post-nuptial settlements to be brokered even before the marriage, something that is still not fully provided for in this jurisdiction. However, in the religious courts of these two faiths, the power to divorce still lies primarily in the hands of the husband.

In Western Europe, Christianity was governed by the Pope in Rome until the Reformation in the 16th century. Until then, Christians believed the biblical teaching that ending a marriage was contrary to God's will. For this reason, not only was divorce forbidden, but post-nuptial settlements were also banned.

This did not mean that the rulers in Christendom always remained tied to an unwanted spouse. Annulments were relatively easy to obtain from the Pope, by arguing that the marriage was void because the parties were too closely related.

Here in England and Wales we were taught in school that the Church's hold over matrimonial matters was broken in 1533 by King Henry VIII's divorce from Catherine of Aragon.

A devout supporter of the papacy, King Henry VIII had expected his marriage to Catherine to be annulled as previously she had been married to his older brother, Prince Arthur, who was now deceased. Unfortunately for the King, Catherine was adamant that her earlier marriage had not been consummated, and she wished to remain Queen of England. She was also the aunt of the Holy Roman Emperor who held control over the Pope, who sided with Catherine, refusing to grant King Henry an annulment.

This transpired during the time of the Reformation, when Protestants were preaching a new interpretation of Christianity across Europe. As some of their teachings allowed for divorce, King Henry decided to sever ties with Rome, appoint himself Head of the Church of England, and persuade the Archbishop of Canterbury to grant him a divorce.

Following the break with Rome, the Ecclesiastical Courts, previously responsible for theological matters, maintained the power to deal with matrimonial issues. However, a divorce could only be obtained by a husband, by way of an Act of Parliament. This meant that divorce was only open to the wealthiest and the most influential male members of society.

Marriage itself was not so well-defined for those who did not own property. Many people were in what were known as common-law marriages – these were permanent relationships, but there had not been a church wedding to mark the union.

By 1857, the year when Parliament introduced the Matrimonial Causes Act, giving women legal standing to use the Civil Court to seek a divorce for the first time, society was rapidly changing. Most of the population was moving from the countryside into the industrialised cities. The first national census, conducted in 1841, demonstrated that women were working alongside men in the factories amid the beginning of a fledgling Women's Movement. Women would not gain full control of their property until the Married Women's Property Act 1882, but by the mid-19th century it became clear to Parliament that there was a need for reform, and that divorce should be made accessible to more people.

Thus began the shift from the total legal subordination of married women, who were slaves in all but name, to sexual equality. No longer would a married woman's person, her property, and her earnings belong to her husband.

During the next 165 years, women would gain freedom from being beaten and raped by their husbands. They would no longer be confined without their consent; they would enjoy joint parental responsibility for their children who could no longer be removed from their care by their husbands – nor would men be able to prevent women from seeing or writing to their offspring.

Same sex couples would be able to marry, and it would become possible for any couple to enter into a civil partnership instead of marriage.

Today no child is in a position whereby he or she can be married under the age of eighteen even with their parents' consent. Arranged marriages abroad or in the jurisdiction for under 18s cannot be entered into by anyone habitually resident in this jurisdiction – these are deemed forced marriages.

Forced marriages have had criminal sanctions since the introduction of the Anti-Social Behaviour Crime and Policing Act of 2014. However, children were not sufficiently protected from being coerced into marriage while under-age (under 18). The Marriage and Civil Partnership (Minimum Age) Act 2022 will now treat the marriage of any child as a forced marriage.

The Matrimonial Causes Act 1857

The 1857 changes came about as a result of men realizing that absolute authority over married women could not be justified by scripture or by the practical realities of family life.

Social historians struggle to fully explain how this transpired, as earlier advocates for social change such as Mary Astell and Mary Wollstencroft were largely ignored by those in power; instead, they created alienation rather than empathy towards the advancement of women's rights. However the 1830s,1840s and 1850s saw a more subtle form of intelligent and unthreatening lobbying by such women as Caroline Norton and Barbara Leigh Smith Bodichon.

The Divorce, Dissolution and Separation Act 2020

On 6 April 2022 Parliament brought into force the Divorce, Dissolution and Separation Act 2020 which allows married parties and civil partners the right to divorce or to end a civil partnership on a no-fault basis. When a marriage or civil partnership goes wrong it is no longer necessary to show or prove the wrongdoing of the other party, or to apportion blame, in order to obtain a divorce, dissolution or separation.

The Act has only nine sections.

A marriage or civil partnership can now be ended on the sole ground of irretrievable breakdown. The old Ecclesiastical names for the stages of a divorce, namely the **Decree Nisi** and the **Decree Absolute**, are replaced by the **Conditional Order** and the **Final Order** – both will be known as Divorce or Dissolution Orders.

Petitioners will now be called Applicants.

The parties to a marriage or civil partnership can apply for a divorce as joint applicants where they both agree that the marriage has irretrievably broken down, albeit a sole applicant can also apply without the other party's consent.

This book explores the journey which led to the new law, and why it is that, for the first time in our history, both sexes have the freedom to live in a marriage or civil partnership with no intervention from the Church and very little from the State, unless they require the help of the courts.

CHAPTER TWO

THE BEGINNING OF THE RIGHT TO DIVORCE

As a society we owe much to several brave reformers and campaigners, who highlighted the need for reform with their writing of novels, pamphlets and other literature. Two of these campaigners are featured below, with a third (A P Herbert) in **CHAPTER THREE.**

Barbara Leigh Smith Bodichon 1827–1891

The illegitimate daughter of a radical Unitarian member of the landed gentry, who had provided her with an endowment which produced an annual income of £300, Barbara Leigh Smith was destined to a different future from most of her female peers as she took up campaigning for women's rights to education and in the home from an early age. As a woman of independent means, she was free from the usual constraints endured by the rest of her sex.

The cousin of Florence Nightingale, she was a forceful character who dedicated her life to working with the poor and to opening up education for women.

By the 1850s, together with a group of friends she established **The Ladies of Langham Place,** a forum to discuss women's rights, one of the first of such movements in the United Kingdom. The novelist George Elliott was a forum member and one of her closest friends.

In 1854, Barbara published a document called a **Brief Summary of the Laws of England Concerning Women,** which would contribute to the introduction of the Matrimonial Causes Act 1857, and more significantly, towards the changes in the way women could hold property, culminating in the Married Women's Property Act 1882.

She herself refrained from marrying her lover Henri Bodichon until the passage of the 1857 Act.

Barbara went on to fight for women's suffrage and the right for women to attend university. She helped Emily Davis establish Hitchen College, which flourished before it became Girton College, of Cambridge University. She was also a talented artist and fought for the right for women to enter the Royal Academy.

Caroline Norton 1808–1877

Born Caroline Elizabeth Sarah Sheridan, this writer and campaigner inherited her grandfather Richard Sheridan's wit and literary talent. To fully understand how this well-connected member of London Society became embroiled in campaigning we need to consider her personal circumstances.

Caroline married barrister George Norton in 1827. Despite his professional qualifications and ostensible standing as a legal professional, George was a financial failure – a gambler and heavy drinker. The couple survived on Caroline's earnings as a writer and her Society connections. By 1836 George's behaviour was more than Caroline could bear, and she left him. Although she continued to earn money from her writing, George continued to take all her earnings, as he was entitled by law to take anything she earned or owned – after all she was his property. Caroline managed to survive through her connections in Society and by running up debts in her husband's name – for which he was liable. As a married woman she was forbidden from entering into any kind of contract.

The situation between the couple worsened when George moved with their sons to Scotland and refused to let Caroline see them. Legally he was entitled to do so, as Caroline had no right to see her children or live with them, if her husband so desired. The children too were regarded as their father's legal property.

Finally, George decided to sue one of Caroline's dearest friends for **Criminal Conversation** – the friend was no other than Lord Melbourne, the then Whig Prime Minister. Although unsuccessful with his claim, made after a failed blackmail attempt by George, it weakened Caroline's status in society and nearly toppled the government. The failed claim did not provide Caroline with a means to divorce George, but the scandal surrounding her case and around other prominent cases at the time, nudged Parliament towards badly-needed reform.

CHAPTER THREE

CRIMINAL CONVERSATION

Open only to husbands, this remedy was banned by the 1857 Act.

A claim for damages following a Criminal Conversation was a claim made by a husband against another man for having sexual intercourse with his wife. Such actions transpired at a time when the criminal courts were no longer pursuing adulterers. After 1746 such prosecutions disappeared from the secular court records. Furthermore, the Ecclesiastical courts (which also possessed the power to punish adultery) were in decline. While adultery was quietly decriminalized, the seduction of a married woman was deemed a form of trespass – hence the civil action given the specific name of Criminal Conversation.

Still regarded as her husband's property, the wife had no right to be a party in proceedings in such cases, nor was she allowed to call witnesses. The parties themselves could not give evidence; however, third parties were summoned to support or refute the allegations; each party could be represented by a barrister who would then make submissions on their behalf. Proceedings were avidly followed by the press and were reported in the finest detail, especially if the parties involved were well-known, and particularly if the details could be documented in graphic and lurid fashion! Such press coverage was particularly hurtful for the unrepresented wife, who was exposed and vulnerable, with no means of defence. Damages awarded by juries were often excessively high, frequently bankrupting the adulterer. By the 1830s, when George Norton pursued his case, they often exceeded £2000 – in today's terms this translates to around £200,000.

Apart from the temptation of receiving excessively high damages another motive for bringing a Criminal Conversation case was that a successful claim enabled a petition for divorce to pass through Parliament.

By 1857 there had been a significant change in society's attitude towards marriage, which may have been influenced by Queen Victoria's successful marriage to Prince Albert. Marriage was now perceived as an institution which provided love and companionship, in which both parties were equally important.

Receiving money for a wife's "dishonour" was increasingly deemed unacceptable. Equally repugnant to most people was the use of a Criminal Conversation claim as a means to obtain a divorce through collusion between the wife's lover and her husband, who in many instances would repay the damages.

Furthermore, many leading figures were uncomfortable with the notion that a wife should accept her husband's adultery, while she could be the victim in a Criminal Conversation case. Educated women were becoming more influential in the argument that they should no longer be treated as possessions owned by their husbands.

Caroline Norton was one of the most influential of those women. Her campaigning undoubtedly influenced Parliament's decision to abolish Criminal Conversation claims in the 1857 Act at the same time as allowing a civil divorce.

The new Act would still allow claims for damages against a correspondent in an adultery claim; this was not abolished until 1970. Moreover, although a husband would be entitled to a divorce if he could prove that his wife had committed adultery, a wife would need to prove adultery and at least one other marital offence (such as cruelty) in order to be granted a divorce. The privilege of being able to remarry following a divorce was only granted to women in 1857.

The Further Growth of Collusion in Divorce Proceedings

By 1923 divorce and remarriage were increasingly considered secular matters between two adults.

Prior to the first World War the Women's Suffrage Movement was on the cusp of winning the vote for women. During the war many women had worked to help the war effort in what was previously considered men's work; the 1920s saw increasing demands for equal rights in all spheres of society.

The vote and the right to stand for Parliament was granted to women over 30 in 1918, while the Equal Franchise Act 1928 gave equal voting rights to all adults 21 years and above.

In this context couples who wanted a divorce needed to adapt the allegations against each other to fit the grounds allowed for divorce, even when there was no considerable animosity between them.

A wife whose husband was living with another woman could prove his adultery, but she had to go through the charade of pretending to invite him back to married life. If he refused she could then proceed to divorce him, based on his adultery and desertion.

Where neither party was committing adultery it was then necessary for one of them to fake an extra-marital affair, which needed to be witnessed while both parties needed to conceal their collusion with each other. If a report of collusion was made about the couple to the King's Proctor, there was a serious risk that the divorce could be aborted.

In 1923 Parliament was persuaded to change the law to allow both parties a divorce based only on the other's adultery. They were not prepared to extend the grounds to cruelty or desertion.

It is hardly surprising that the issue of collusion then became even more of a problem.

A P Herbert

By 1937 pressure for reform was being driven by independent MP Alan Patrick Herbert (known as AP Herbert), an ardent law reformer who was also a published novelist and poet.

To bolster his arguments for the need for reform, in 1934 he wrote Holy Deadlock, a satirical novel which depicted a young couple who no longer wished to remain married, and separated from each other due to incompatibility, not because of adultery.

In the book, the wife meets another man who cannot be named as an adulterer, otherwise he would lose his job. The husband agrees to provide false evidence of adultery, and eventually a decree nisi of divorce is granted, but the wife is then discovered to have spent the night with her fiancé. An acquaintance reports the wife to the King's Proctor and the divorce is halted. Neither party can then remarry.

A lawyer in the novel describes the case as an ordinary English one, based on collusion, one of thousands of similar cases a year. Everything runs smoothly, he adds, until people begin telling the truth. The book became a best seller, with the hypocrisy it exposed boosting the author's Private Members Bill, which introduced new grounds for divorce based on desertion and cruelty. Although it ended the need to prove adultery without collusion, it started the trend by which the respondent fails to defend the petition lodged against them. This only ended on 6 April 2022, with the advent of the Divorce Dissolution and Separation Act 2022. This phenomenon usually transpired out of pragmatism in the belief that there was no point defending a petition by filing an answer if the marriage was in any case over, and also because of the cost of and publicity surrounding defended proceedings.

CHAPTER FOUR

THE YEARS 1937–1969: PRE-WWII TO MODERN TIMES

There is little doubt that World War II had a profound effect on family life.

Once again, a large percentage of the male population was deployed to fight overseas. Women were mobilised to undertake their work at home, with some also fighting at the front.

Many marriages suffered from the enforced separations caused by the war, and sadly many husbands did not return from the front. After 1945, and the end of WWII, husbands filed a larger number of petitions than usual alleging adultery. Marital breakdowns citing other reasons were also not uncommon.

The records show that during the 1950s the divorce rate slowed down; for a short period, longer and more successful marriages than previously were recorded. This may be accounted for by the rapidly increasing life expectancy of both partners, following the creation of the National Health Service and ever more discoveries in medical practice. It also reflected a nostalgic period of looking back to what was perceived as a more stable way of life before the war.

It is worth remembering that for most families prior to the 1950s the premature death of one parent or the other was not unusual, with children brought up by step-parents as often as they are in modern times.

Today, divorce can indeed fracture family life, but it is a myth to believe that families successfully remained as a united unit before the 20th century, when it was so difficult to obtain a divorce. A high percentage of families were affected by frequent deaths in childbirth experienced by women, and by the crippling effect of large-scale warfare on two generations of the male population. In reality there were far fewer stable marriages than the nostalgia of the 1950s would have us believe.

By the end of the post-war era other factors affected the stability of marriage. Increasing numbers of couples sought to end their marriages, only to discover that they were faced with an expensive and humiliating process if they wished to forge ahead with proceedings.

There followed a number of statutes during the 1960s to reform the law, culminating in the introduction of the Matrimonial Causes Act 1973.

The Matrimonial Causes Act 1973 (MCA 1973)

In 1973 this piece of legislation amalgamated the reforms of the late 1960s, with its introduction considered very radical. The former grounds of divorce, based only on the fault of the other party without collusion were abandoned, and it was no longer necessary to attend court for the hearing of a decree nisi unless the respondent filed an answer to the petition.

Section1 of the Act sets out the following:

> "…a petition for divorce may be presented to the court by either party to the marriage on the ground that the marriage has broken down irretrievably."

Although this was the only ground, it was then restricted by the need for support by one of the five facts, as set out in section 1(2):

a) that the respondent has committed adultery and the petitioner finds it intolerable to live with the respondent.

b) that the respondent has behaved in such a way that the petitioner cannot reasonably be expected to live with the respondent

c) that the respondent has deserted the petitioner for a continuous period of at least two years preceding the presentation of the petition

d) that the parties to the marriage have lived apart for a continuous period of at least two years immediately preceding the presentation of the petition (hereinafter in this Act referred to as "two years separation"), and the respondent consents to the decree being granted

e) that the parties to the marriage have lived apart for a continuous period of at least five years immediately preceding the presentation of the petition (hereinafter in this Act referred to as "five years separation")

In 1966 the recommendations made to Parliament by both the Archbishop of Canterbury's Group in its report "Putting Asunder," and that of the Law Commission, "The Field of Choice," were in favour of introducing no fault divorce.

Both these reports highlighted that 93 per cent of petitions for divorce at that time were undefended – in other words, divorces were obtained by collusion and with mutual consent.

In 1969, the MP Leonard Abse, who had already launched the bill leading to the decriminalisation of homosexuality with the Sexual Offences Act 1967, introduced a bill to convert the new idea of no-fault divorce into law. His bill allowed for the one and only ground of irretrievable breakdown of marriage, contingent on proof of adultery, cruelty, desertion, two years' separation (with consent) or five years' separation, (no consent necessary).

Abse's Bill was passed in 1969 as the Divorce Reform Act 1969 and was then consolidated by the Matrimonial Causes Act 1973, which again allowed irretrievable breakdown of the marriage to be the one and only ground for divorce.

Following these reforms, what then became clear from the number of divorces published per annum, was that the old habit of relying on the blame of one party for a marriage's demise in fact did continue, although it was possible to wait for two years (with the consent of the other party) to introduce a petition on a no-fault basis.

There is no doubt that the reforms culminating in the Matrimonial Causes Act 1973 transpired at a time of seismic change in social norms pertaining to the role of women both in the workplace and in the home. It is no coincidence that three years earlier the Equal Pay Act 1970 was introduced, which was then followed by the Sex Discrimination Act 1975.

In 1960 the number of divorces in England and Wales totalled approximately 24,000. By 2020 this figure had risen to 103,592 (slightly down from 2019). Although the number of divorces has swelled over the past fifty years, as we have already considered, when looking at family stability, it is important to take into account the high adult mortality rate well into the 20th century, with women frequently dying in childbirth and young men being killed in warfare. However, after World War II, statistics show that following a sharp spike in husbands' petitions alleging adultery, in the 1950s there was a period of family stability. Nostalgia may have played a part, with people longing to return to a more traditional past, but by 1960 society began to return to the changes that sparked in the 1920s.

If this is looked at statistically, the proportion of marital dissolution caused by death was as frequent as that by divorce today. In other words, marriages then lasted no longer than they do today; hence the "wicked stepmother" appearing so regularly in children's fairy tales. It is nostalgia that drives the belief that the breakdown of the institution of marriage is the root of all society's ills, as such stability has rarely existed.

CHAPTER FIVE

THE NEED FOR REFORM POST-1973

Unfortunately, the pious hope of the reformers, that by introducing two years' separation with consent, as a fact to establish the ground for divorce would be most commonly relied on, did not tally with the wishes of most divorcing couples. Most wanted a divorce immediately.

Petitions following 1973 were predominately issued citing a respondent's adultery or unreasonable behaviour. This was despite the courts making it clear from shortly after the reforms' introduction, that such allegations would rarely, if ever, affect the parties' financial settlements.

This was all clearly explained by Lord Denning in the case of *Wachtel-v-Wachtel [1973] EWCA*:

> "When Parliament in 1857 introduced divorce by the Courts of Law it based it on the doctrine of the matrimonial offence. This affected all that followed. If a person was the guilty party in a divorce suit it went hard with him or her. It affected so many things. The custody of the children depended on it, as did the award of maintenance, to say nothing of the standing in society. So serious were the consequences that divorce suits were contested at great length and at much cost."

He then went on to dismiss the husband's arguments that Mrs Wachtel's financial claim should be reduced because of her conduct, stating that:

> "In the financial adjustments consequent upon the dissolution of a marriage which is irretrievably broken down, the imposition of financial penalties ought seldom to find a place."

Following the introduction of the Matrimonial Causes Act 1973, a several decisions were made by the courts, on the nature of unreasonable behaviour, which was interpreted as being subjective. Petitions succeeded with such allegations as lack of socialising together, sleeping separately, working long hours and failing to help in the home. Allegations of a more serious nature were also relied on, such as physical and mental abuse. Parties were encouraged by the system to come up with a series of often hurtful and/or humiliating allegations to ensure that petitions went through successfully. In addition, they were rarely contested, despite respondents having the right to file an answer.

Answers were rarely filed because the respondent only had to acknowledge the breakdown of the marriage on the form of Acknowledgement of Service, by indicating they did not wish to defend proceedings and that they did not oppose the granting of a decree nisi. An admission of adultery was necessary if this fact was relied on, but admissions of unreasonable behaviour were not required.

If an Answer was filed there was a directions appointment listed, in which the respondent was encouraged to compromise and withdraw the same by the court. This was because by filing the petition, the petitioner was demonstrating that the marriage had broken down and that the cost of a fully contested hearing would be wholly disproportionate, given that the blame for the breakdown would be irrelevant in financial proceedings. Very few cases proceeded to trial. Many were compromised by the respondent filing a cross-petition and each party being granted a decree nisi.

What Lord Denning had decided in the Wachtel case, was followed by the courts when considering that the parties' financial applications and conduct was rarely relevant. The petition's contents could, and often did, increase the bitterness between the parties, but the divorce proceedings themselves were not where the parties generally accrued high fees. Fees mounted because of the parties' inability to settle financial matters, and of more concern to the courts, their inability to agree arrangements for their children. The allegations in the petition could often influence the parties' conduct in these proceedings.

In 1984 The Matrimonial and Family Proceedings Act allowed couples to petition for divorce after one year of marriage, whereas previously they needed to wait for three years. Following this change, by way of an amendment to section 3 MCA 1973, there was a significant increase in petitions.

By the early 1990s the high rate of divorce was causing panic among some MPs and the then Prime Minister Margaret Thatcher's government. Divorced mothers and single parents were identified as bearing the responsibility for the increasing cost of social funding. The Child Support Act 1991 was introduced with the initial intent of forcing those on Income Support to make the other parent pay and for their benefits to be reduced accordingly. This policy proved to be a failure, and its implementation wasted public money, but it did have all party support and reflected Parliament's concern about the state of the family.

In this context serious consideration was given to reforming the MCA1973 to slow down the process of marital breakdowns and encourage potential divorcees to reflect on the wisdom of embarking on the divorce process.

At the same time the need to eradicate the collusion created by the system was also recognized by the introduction of a no-fault system. Family law practitioners, both at the Bar and through the Solicitors'

Family Law Association (now Resolution) had started a proactive campaign for the reform of section 1 of the MCA 1973, by removing the requisite to blame the other party with accusations of adultery, unreasonable behaviour or desertion, as set out in section 1(2).

The Family Law Act 1996

When enacted, Part II of the Family Law Act 1996, which came into effect in 1999 contained a new regime for obtaining a divorce.

There was to be only one ground for divorce: irretrievable breakdown of the marriage, meaning that all divorces would be on a no-fault basis.

However, a petition for divorce could not commence unless the parties had separated for 18 months and had attended compulsory marriage counselling. In addition, couples were required to undergo a period of reflection before starting proceedings. Before the divorce could be finalised, the couple would need to agree on financial needs and settlements, as well arrangements for and wishes on the part of any children in the mix concerning their future and subsequent arrangements.

Although the Act remains in force, the practicalities and the cost of introducing such a regime meant that the statutory instruments required to change the then Family Proceedings Rules were never implemented, and Part II has never been activated.

In effect, despite Parliament's attempt to allow for no fault divorce from as early as 1999, until 6 April 2022, when the new Act became law, petitions continued to rely predominately on allegations of adultery or unreasonable behaviour, despite constant lobbying for change, especially by Resolution.

Not only would it have been very expensive to implement Part II of the Family Law Act, but also any attempts to impose counselling would have been unpopular in the eyes of the public. Therefore, the use of blame to enable divorce would continue – until 6 April 2022 – tempered by the knowledge that financial outcomes would not be affected.

Other Issues Affecting Family Life post-1999

It is worth recalling that by the end of the 20th century the number of couples who chose to live together and start families without getting married marked another significant societal transformation. By 2017, 48.1 percent of children in England and Wales were born to single or cohabiting parents, demonstrating that a significant number of families are avoiding the legislation which governs the breakdown of family life.

As noted by Coleridge J in *K-v-K [2005]2FLR 468:*

> "In the 35 years since the enactment *(of the Matrimonial Causes Act 1973, L.C.),* a social revolution has taken place. The concept of cohabitation is now as normal, common place and acceptable as marriage. At every level of society and amongst all adult age groups, people cohabit without a second thought. It carries no social stigma whatever."

While many couples do opt to get married after the birth of their children, it is clear that any stigma attached to illegitimacy, and any possible fear of religious sanctions has all but been eradicated.

What is of concern is that unless couples living together in such circumstances have had contracts and trusts set up to protect their rights, they are not protected by the fiction of "a common law marriage," and they are required to litigate in the civil courts to sort out any property held between them. There is no obligation to maintain one another following the breakdown of a relationship, albeit they can make claims for their children pursuant to the Children Act 1989 for financial support where the Child Maintenance Service (formerly known as the Child Support Agency) does not have jurisdiction.

Civil Partnerships

At the same time, and contrary to the trend veering away from marriage between heterosexual couples, single sex partners were demanding the right to marry. Initially, Parliament was only prepared to allow them to enter into civil partnerships by introducing the Civil Partnership Act 2004, which came into effect on 5 December 2005. From then, same-sex couples were afforded the right to register a civil partnership and thereby enjoy most rights and obligations alike, as were applicable to married partners.

The Matrimonial Causes Act 1973 was amended to allow for the dissolution of civil partnerships.

To end such a relationship, a petition could be filed for dissolution of the civil partnership. To prove irretrievable breakdown of such a partnership, the facts relied on were similar to those required for a divorce from marriage, namely: unreasonable behaviour, including infidelity, desertion for two years or more, two years' separation with consent, or five years' separation with no consent necessary.

The Marriage (Same Sex Couples) Act 2013

Many same sex couples regarded the Civil Partnership Act as discriminatory and continued to campaign for the right to marry. Their campaign was successful, giving way to the introduction of the

Marriage (Same Sex Couples) Act 2013 on 17 July 2013. The first same sex marriage took place on 29 March 2014. In the event of a religious organisation allowing same sex marriages, couples may participate in the relevant religious ceremony. It is also possible to convert a civil partnership into a marriage, with divorces granted, if necessary, pursuant to Section 1 of the Matrimonial Causes Act 1973.

Ironically, while same sex couples continued to fight for the right to marry, heterosexual couples wishing to formalise their relationships with a lifelong commitment, campaigned for the right to register as civil partners. This right was extended to them when the Civil Partnership (Opposite Sex Couples) Regulations 2019 were brought into force on 31 December 2019.

CHAPTER SIX

OWENS -V- OWENS [2018] EWCA CIV (182) / UKSC41

Since the Matrimonial Causes Act 1973, the least expensive and litigious part of the process for most couples involved in divorce proceedings, was obtaining a Decree Nisi of Divorce.

The expense arose from the financial proceedings and disputes concerning the children.

In most cases, petitions were acknowledged by respondents indicating that they did not intend to defend. There were minor skirmishes around costs but very few Answers were filed and even fewer cases progressed to trial.

While a Decree Absolute of Divorce could be obtained by the petitioner six weeks and one day after the granting of the Decree Nisi, parties generally waited to finalise the Decree Absolute after financial arrangements were determined.

Respondents who did not wish to wait could apply for a Decree Absolute after three months following the period of six weeks and a day. Several contested applications have been reported. In most cases the respondent would have been most likely to succeed with their application. An exception would be if the petitioner would lose a benefit, usually under a pension scheme, if the Decree Absolute was granted before the finances had been settled.

This was known as a "Special Circumstance." See *Dart-v-Dart [1996] 2FLR286.*

Where Butler-Sloss LJ (as she then was) said in the Court of Appeal:

> "In the normal course of events he would be able to obtain the decree absolute, unless the wife is able to show "Special Circumstances" to defer it. At the end of the day, it is an exercise of the discretion of the trial judge, that exercise of discretion weights the granting of the decree absolute against the Special Circumstances very heavily in favour of the grant. It is not a balancing exercise in the ordinary sense."

In the case of Thacker-v-Thacker [2016] EWHC2488 the wife was the petitioner, and indicated that she would not be applying for the decree absolute until her financial claim had been resolved. When Mr Thacker applied for a decree absolute he was refused, because Mrs Thacker was able to demonstrate that she would be heavily impacted financially as soon as the decree absolute was made. That is, she demonstrated Special Circumstances.

By 2018 it was however the case that the Supreme Court had never had cause to consider the way in which the ground for divorce of irretrievable breakdown of marriage (Section 1 Matrimonial Causes Act 1973) was proved by one of the five facts set out in Section 1(2), in particular the fact of unreasonable behaviour.

Mr and Mrs Owens were a couple who became embroiled in a fully-contested divorce. Married in 1978 they had two adult children; in 2018 Mrs Owens was 68 years old with Mr Owens 12 years older at the age of 80.

By 2012 Mrs Owens believed her marriage had broken down and was given legal advice about a possible divorce in June of the same year; by November she had started an extra-marital affair. In 2015, after 37 years of marriage, Mrs Owens left the marital home.

Her next step was to file a petition for divorce seeking to prove that the marriage had broken down irretrievably due to Mr Owens's unreasonable behaviour. Supporting allegations included: Mr Owens prioritised work over home life; he did not demonstrate love, attention or affection; he suffered from mood swings, causing frequent arguments which were both distressing and hurtful; and he was unpleasant and disparaging about his wife in public.

Had Mr Owens not defended the petition, Mrs Owens would have been granted a Decree Nisi. Unfortunately for Mrs Owens, her husband did not think that the marriage had irretrievably broken down and he filed an Answer to her petition.

His Answer accepted that the marriage had not been emotionally intense, but he thought that he and Mrs Owens had learned to "rub along." His Answer was supported by the trial judge who determined that Mrs Owens could not show that it was unreasonable to live with Mr Owens, and he dismissed the petition. On appealing the decision, the Court of Appeal agreed with the trial judge. Mrs Owens was then granted leave to appeal to the Supreme Court, which unanimously upheld the Court of Appeal's decision and dismissed the appeal, sending shock waves through the legal community.

Lead judge Lord Wilson acknowledged that defended proceedings were "exceedingly rare," and upheld the trial judge's finding that the marriage had broken down. He went on to explain that:

> "When applying s.1(2).....by reference to allegations of behaviour,'' the court needed "to determine what the respondent did or did not do," and that it also needed "to assess the effect which the behaviour had upon this particular petitioner...," and then "make an evaluation as to whether....an expectation that the petitioner should continue to live with the respondent would be reasonable.''

Although the petition remained dismissed on this basis, Lord Wilson went on to say that: "The majority invites Parliament to consider replacing a law which denies Mrs Owens a divorce in the present circumstances."

The Aftermath

In September 2018 Justice Secretary David Gauke launched a consultation proposing that Parliament should urgently explore the removal of wrongdoing allegations from the petition, and the right to file an Answer from the process of divorce. His reasoning was that the divorce laws were out of touch with modern life, and that: "the blame game that currently exists helps nobody. It creates unnecessary antagonism and anxiety at an already trying time for the couple."

A response to the consultation was published on 9 April 2019 with the government announcing on the same day that it would be introducing No Fault Divorce. This was widely welcomed by the legal profession. The organization Resolution stated: "We welcome these proposals …with this new legislation, finally our divorce laws will be brought up to date, will help divorcing couples and, most importantly, any children they may have, will avoid unnecessary conflict."

CHAPTER SEVEN

DIVORCE, DISSOLUTION AND SEPARATION ACT 2020

The nine sections of the Act amend both the Matrimonial Causes Act 1973 and the Civil Partnership Act 2004. This is summarised below.

Section 1 of the Matrimonial Causes Act 1973 is substituted by the following provisions:

1. "Divorce on breakdown of marriage"

1) Subject to section 3, either or both parties to a marriage may apply to the court for an order (a "divorce order")

which dissolves the marriage, on the ground that the marriage has broken down irretrievably.

2) An application under subsection (1) must be accompanied by a statement by the applicant or applicants that the marriage has broken down irretrievably

3) The court dealing with an application under subsection (1) must:

a) take the statement to be conclusive evidence that the marriage has broken down irretrievably, and,

b) make a divorce order.

4) A divorce order:

a) is, in the first instance a conditional order, and

b) may not be made final before the end of a period of six weeks and a day from the making of the conditional order

(5) The court may not make a conditional order unless:

a) in the case of an application that is to proceed as an application by one party to the marriage only, that party has confirmed to the court that they wish the application to continue, or

b) in the case of an application that is to proceed as an application by both parties to the marriage, those parties have confirmed to the court that they wish the application to continue; and a party may not give confirmation for the purpose of this subsection before the end of the period of 20 weeks from the start of proceedings."

Subsections (6) – (10) deal with implementation and procedure.

Section 2 deals with Judicial Separation where the amendments to Section 17 of the Matrimonial Causes Act 1973 follow those made for divorce.

A Judicial Separation is replaced by a Judicial Separation Order. An application can be made by one or both parties to the marriage without needing to allege any fact in support.

Section 3 deals with the dissolution of a civil partnership where the amendments made to section 44 of The Civil Partnership Act 2004 allow for joint applications, and follow the amendments in section 1 above, by removing the facts previously relied on to show irretrievable breakdown.

Section 4 provides that Section 37A will now state that:

> "1) Every dissolution order:
>
> > a) is in the first instance a conditional order, and
> >
> > b) may not be made final before the end of the period of 6 weeks from the making of the conditional order (the "first prescribed period")
>
> 2) The court may not make a conditional order unless:
>
> > a) In the case of an application that is to proceed as an application by one civil partner only, that person has confirmed to the court that they wish to continue, or
> >
> > b) in the case of an application that is to proceed as an application by both civil partners, those persons have confirmed to the court that they wish the to continue"

Section 5 provides that Section 56 will allow joint applications for a Separation Order and the factual grounds are removed.

Sections 60-9 are procedural as is the Schedule to the Act.

In Part 1 of the Schedule there are further amendments to the Matrimonial Causes Act 1973 (MCA) which are headed as minor and consequential.

It remains the case that an application for a divorce cannot be made in the first year of marriage as Section 3 MCA remains unaltered.

A divorce is no longer precluded by a previous judicial separation, nor can grounds of hardship be pleaded to delay a divorce.

It is not necessary to file a certificate of reconciliation.

The power for the Queen's Proctor to intervene pursuant to section 8 remains in force.

The appropriate amendments to the Matrimonial Causes Act 1973 regarding nullity are also dealt with by the Schedule.

The New Procedure post 6 April 2022

The new Form D8 can be found in the Annex. However, if the applicant is legally represented most applications must now be applied for through the HMCTS Solicitor Portal for a Divorce or Dissolution.

Guidance may be found online at: https://www.gov.uk/guidance/myhmcts-online-case-management-for-legal-professionals as to how to set up a portal.

The link is also on the D8 itself.

Litigants in person are encouraged to file online but they are able to file on paper if they prefer to do so. The link is found via http://www.gov.uk/divorce/file-for-divorce

With the D8 it is necessary to file:

a) A marriage or civil partnership certificate or certified copy. A photocopy will not be acceptable.

b) If the certificate is not in English, a translation by a notary public or authenticated by a statement of truth by the person who undertook the translation must also be filed.

c) The court fee, current details of which may be found at https://www.gov.uk/government/collections/court-and-tribunal-forms The fee, currently £593.00, is paid on the digital server by the applicant.

Details for those eligible for a fee remission can be found at https://www.gov.uk/get-help-with-court-fees.

Joint Applications

Section 1(1) allows for both parties to make an application for a divorce.

Where a joint application is made, the parties will be known as Applicant 1 and Applicant 2.

It is now possible for the same solicitor to represent both applicants. Under such circumstances, the D8 should be filed on paper. In the event of a joint application either party can elect to pay the fee.

Help with fees for joint applications requires both parties to prove that their resources are low enough to qualify for such assistance.

When applying for a Conditional Order or a Final Order a joint application may be converted into a sole application.

A sole application may not be converted into a joint application at any stage.

When applying for a Conditional Order and to convert to being a sole applicant, a copy of the application should be sent to the other applicant **at the same time** as the application is made.

Before applying for the Final Order, if it is intended to convert the application to a single application, notice must be given fourteen days beforehand to the other applicant.

Service

(PART 6 FPR as amended by the Family Procedure (Amendment) Rules 2022).

(See Appendix)

The Family Procedure Rules 2010 are amended so that:

a) Service within the jurisdiction will be effected by the court

b) The applicant can apply to effect service

c) Service can be effected by email to the respondent's last known usual email address, ie the email actively used by them for personal emails. Business email addresses should be avoided wherever possible.

d) Where service is effected by email it is also necessary to notify the party served by post that the application has been served by email, and to provide a link to enable that email to be viewed

e) If the applicant only has the respondent's email address, an application is required for leave for service to be effected by email only

f) Where the Court fails to effect the postal notification, an alternative address can be provided. If this fails, the Court will not try to serve for a third time.

g) If the respondent lives overseas, service will not be undertaken by the court. When submitting a D8, **Solicitor Service** needs to be requested. It is then necessary to comply with Chapter 4 Part 6.41A FPR as amended.

h) Where the applicant serves the application, it must be effected before 12 midnight on the day, 28 days after the date of issue. It is possible to apply for an extension of time, which should be made within the 28-day period.

Acknowledging Service

An Acknowledgement of Service is served with a sole application upon the respondent, who is given 14 days to complete the form and return it to the court.

The respondent no longer has the right to file an Answer to the proceedings, unless:

a) The respondent does not accept that the court has jurisdiction

b) The validity of the marriage or civil partnership is disputed

c) The marriage or civil partnership has already ended

An Answer must be filed and served within 21 days of the date when the Acknowledgement of Service is required to be filed. The fee is currently £245.00.

Cross Applications

If a respondent wishes to file their own application they will need to apply to the court for permission to do so, unless the application has already been dismissed. This allows for a respondent to proceed to obtain their divorce in a case where the applicant has failed to pursue matters.

Conditional Orders

As long as the time for filing the Acknowledgement of Service has expired, and an Answer has not been filed, a Conditional Order can be applied for 20 weeks after the issue of the Application.

Final Orders

The Final Order can be applied for six weeks and one day after the pronouncement of the Conditional Order. When applying more than 12 months later, it is still necessary to explain to the court the reason for the delay in obtaining the Final Order.

In the event of a joint application, and one party wishes to make a sole application for a Final Order, they must give the other applicant 14 days' notice and file a Certificate of Service confirming that such notice has been given.

Section 10(2)&(3) MCA 1973

This section now provides as follows:

> "...where a conditional order has been made in favour of one party or both parties, but one has since withdrawn from the application, and the respondent has applied to the Court for consideration of their financial position after the divorce, the Court must not make the Divorce Order final, unless it is satisfied that:
>
> a) The applicant should not be required to make any financial provision for the respondent, or

b) The financial provision made by the applicant for the respondent is reasonable and fair, or the best that can be made in the circumstances.

The court must consider all the circumstances, including:

a) The age, health, conduct, earning capacity, financial resources and financial obligations of each party to the marriage, and:

b) The financial position of the respondent having regard to the divorce, it is likely to be after the death of the applicant, should that person die first

The court may still make the divorce final:

a) If it appears that there are circumstances making it desirable that the Order should be made final without delay

b) The court has obtained a satisfactory undertaking from the Applicant that they will make such financial provision for the respondent as the Court may approve.

Contrary to encouraging the parties to resolve their financial needs through ADR, it may become necessary to advise the issue of an application on Form A, to enable a delay to the granting of the Final Order.

The application to delay the Final Order will need to be made quickly, preferably before the end of the six-week period.

The necessity of making such an application should be discussed with a respondent upon taking instructions. It is likely that the case law relating to "Special Circumstances" in delaying the Decree Absolute will be cited in future litigation arising from these amendments. (See CHAPTER SIX *Dart-v-Dart*)

Section 10 A (1) MCA 1973

This Section provided that where a couple were married in accordance with "the usages of the Jews" or other religious usages and these prescribe final dissolution, an application can be made under Section 10 A (2) for an order that stays the grant of a decree absolute. The stay will continue until the court is satisfied by a declaration of both parties that the marriage is also dissolved in accordance with those "[Jewish or other] usages." See Rule 7.30.

It is assumed that this Rule will be extended to enable a Jewish wife, in particular, to delay the making of a final order, albeit this is not currently clear under Rule 7.30.

Costs

There has been no change in the rules. When an application is in dispute – eg, an issue over jurisdiction, Cost Orders can be made against the unsuccessful party.

While it is possible in an undisputed case to pursue a Part 18 application for a Cost Order in an undisputed case, its success is unlikely. In practice, it would be preferable for the parties to reach an agreement on costs before the issue of the application.

CHAPTER EIGHT

THE FUTURE

For the first time in history in the jurisdiction of England and Wales it is possible to end a marriage or civil partnership between two adults without one party taking the blame for the marriage breakdown. Collusion is no longer necessary for a couple to be free of each other without waiting for a two-year separation.

Many may see these changes as furthering the breakdown of family life as we once knew it, and they may grieve the fact that marriage is no longer treated as a sacrament by the courts. Such a view does need to be put into context.

In this jurisdiction many of our religious bodies have the authority to marry couples, although some are not prepared to marry same sex couples. Thus any couple wishing to engage in a religious marriage service may do so if their religious body is licensed to marry them and is willing to do so. It is then up to that couple to abide by the vows they pledge to each other. They are free to consider these vows as binding with the marriage recognised in this jurisdiction. They are not obliged to engage in a separate civil marriage ceremony, which is the case in many other jurisdictions. For example, in France only the civil marriage is valid.

Conversely, when marriage and civil partnerships fail, the parties that make up the relationships no longer have to justify the breakdown using harmful allegations that only add to the bitterness and acrimony surrounding marriage breakdowns.

The so-called sanctity of marriage was always debatable when one party to the union was regarded as a chattel with no rights.

Furthermore, until the end of the 19th century there were as many, if not more, children living in single parent homes or with a stepparent as today, due to the high adult mortality rate in bygone years.

This situation was made worse by World Wars I and II in the last century.

It is hoped that the new provisions for divorce will ease the bitterness surrounding the breakdown of relationships, without encouraging people to embark on the procedure for frivolous reasons.

One problem that has already been identified is it will now take at least six months and a day to be granted the Final Order, and new section 10(2)&(3) provisions may also be used to delay matters. At the time of publication, it is still too early to assess how many cases will be further delayed by the new section 10(2)&(3) of MCA1973.

There is still a significant minority of relationships with children in the mix, for whom the issue of divorce or dissolution is irrelevant. The need for legislation for such couples is widely recognised but appears unlikely to transpire in the near future. Perhaps the availability of a civil partnership instead of marriage will encourage more couples to formalise their relationships, and maybe the ability to divorce or obtain a dissolution on a no-fault basis will encourage more marriages and civil partnerships.

In the meantime, it is important for those dealing with property purchases and transfers for unmarried couples to provide them with the correct advice to avoid a negligence claim for failing to do so.

Further reading: the Family Court Practice 2022, Lexis Nexis; Road to Divorce England 1530-1987, Lawrence Stone.

APPENDIX ONE

FORM D8

From:
https://www.gov.uk/government/publications/form-d8-application-for-a-divorce-dissolution-or-to-apply-for-a-judicial-separation-order

You can apply online
Divorce – www.gov.uk/apply-for-divorce
Dissolution – www.gov.uk/end-civil-partnership

Application for a divorce or dissolution (ending a civil partnership)

HMCTS USE ONLY

You can only make an application for divorce or dissolution if you have been in your marriage or civil partnership for at least one year.

If there are exceptional reasons why your application should be dealt with urgently then please set those reasons out in a covering letter.

Legal representatives are required to apply digitally through the My HMCTS Solicitor Portal for a Divorce or Dissolution. You can find more information at: https://www.gov.uk/guidance/myhmcts-online-case-management-for-legal-professionals

Section 1 – Your application

1.1 What application are you making?

☐ **Divorce** on the ground that the marriage has broken down irretrievably

☐ **Dissolution** on the ground that the civil partnership has broken down irretrievably

1.2 Are you applying as a sole applicant or joint applicants?

☐ **A sole application** – I am applying on my own.

You will complete this application on your own before you submit it to the court. The court will send a copy of your application to your spouse/civil partner.

You will be referred to as the sole applicant, and your spouse/civil partner will be referred to as the respondent in this application.

☐ **A joint application** – We are applying together.

You and your spouse/civil partner will complete this application jointly before you submit to the court.

You will be referred to as applicant 1 and your spouse/civil partner as applicant 2 in this application.

Applicant 2 must complete section 3 and the statement of truth.

Relationship support and child arrangements
Where it may be helpful (and safe) to recieve relationship support, you can find information at: https://www.nhs.uk/Service-Search/other-services/Relationship%20counselling/LocationSearch/400

You can also find information on making child arrangements if you divorce or separate at: https://www.gov.uk/looking-after-children-divorce

Note: If you entered into a religious marriage as well as a civil marriage, these divorce proceedings may not dissolve the religious part of your marriage. It is important that you contact the relevant religious authority and seek further guidance if you are unsure.

Note 1.2: How you divide your money and property is dealt with separately. You may wish to consider taking legal advice.

It should not affect your decision on whether to do a sole or a joint application.

Any application for costs should be made using form **D11** application notice. This is available on the gov.uk website.

D8 Application for a divorce or dissolution (ending a civil partnership) (04.22)

1.3 What documents are you supplying to support your application?

- [ ] Your marriage or civil partnership certificate or a certified copy of the certificate from where you got married or entered into a civil partnership (a photocopy will **not** be accepted).

- [ ] A translation that has been certified by a notary public or authenticated by a statement of truth by the person who did the translation. This should be provided if your marriage or civil partnership certificate (or a similar document issued under the law in the country you registered your marriage or civil partnership) is not in English.

For marriages/civil partnerships in England and Wales you can order a copy of the certificate at www.gro.gov.uk/gro/content/certificates. You will need to pay for each copy.

In cases of urgency it may be possible for you to make an application to allow you to deliver the original or a certified copy of the marriage/civil partnership certificate to the court at a later date, if the document is unavailable. To do this, you will need to complete and file the **D11** application notice. This is available at https://www.gov.uk/government/publications/form-d11-application-notice

Section 2 – About you
(the sole applicant or applicant 1)

2.1 Full name of the sole applicant or applicant 1

First name(s)

Middle name(s)

Last name

Is this either your married name or the name shown on your marriage or civil partnership certificate?

☐ Yes

☐ No. Please attach your change of name deed/statutory declaration or if this is not applicable, explain why your name has changed

Note 2.1: This can be different to the one on your marriage or civil partnership certificate. This can be your last name, your spouse/civil partner's last name or a double barrelled last name that combines the two. If you have changed your name, other than through your marriage, since you got married you must attach a copy of your change of name deed or otherwise explain why your name has changed.

2.2 Do you wish to keep your contact details confidential from your spouse or civil partner?

☐ Yes. Please keep my details confidential.

☐ No

Note 2.2: If you do not wish to disclose your contact details to the respondent, please tick 'Yes' and complete question 2.3 below.

Page 3

2.3 What is your address and contact details?

Building and street

Second line of address

Town or city

County (optional)

Country

Postcode

Phone number (if you have one)

Email (if you have one)

Note 2.3: You should give a home address in the UK, if you have one. The court will send papers to your home address, or you can provide a business address in the UK. If you want to supply an address outside of the UK, different rules may apply about documents being sent to you. You may wish to seek legal advice.

Remember information contained in this form will be sent to your spouse/civil partner. If you do not want them to know your current contact details, please make sure you have ticked 'Yes' at question 2.2, the court will not disclose these details.

If you have not provided an email address, the court will send a copy of the issued application to your postal address.

2.4 Do you have a solicitor?

☐ Yes. **Complete the following questions (2.5 – 2.8)**

☐ No. **Go to Section 3.**

Note 2.4: For a solicitor completing this application: references to 'solicitor' in this form includes any person who, for the purposes of the Legal Services Act 2007, is an authorised person in relation to an activity which constitutes the conduct of litigation (within the meaning of that Act)

2.5 The solicitor's name

2.6 The solicitor's reference number (if applicable)

2.7 Name of the solicitor's firm

2.8 Address of solicitor's firm

Building and street

Second line of address

Town or city

County (optional)

Country

Postcode

DX address (if applicable)

Phone number

Email

Section 3 – About the respondent or applicant 2

If you are applying as a sole applicant, complete this section with the respondent's details.

If applying jointly, applicant 2 must complete this section. Applicant 1 should continue to complete the form at Section 4.

3.1 Full name

First name(s)

Middle name(s)

Last name

Note: For applicant 2, this can be different to the one on your marriage or civil partnership certificate. This can be your last name, your spouse/civil partner's last name or a double barrelled last name that combines the two.

If you have changed your name, other than through your marriage, since you got married you must attach a copy of your change of name deed or otherwise explain why your name has changed.

3.2 Is this either the married name or the name shown on the marriage or civil partnership certificate?

☐ Yes

☐ No. Please attach the change of name deed/statutory declaration or if this is not applicable, explain why the name has changed

3.3 What is the address of the respondent or applicant 2?

Building and street

Second line of address

Town or city

County (optional)

Country

Postcode

Phone number (if there is one)

Note 3.3: Where the application is to be served by the court this will be served by email with a notice confirming service sent to the respondent's postal address.

Please insert the respondent's usual email address or an email address provided by the respondent for service (for example, their solicitor's email address). You should avoid using a work email address, as this may not be confidential.

Email (if there is one)

☐ For the respondent's email address only – I confirm that to the best of my knowledge only the respondent has access to the above email account

If this is a joint application please go to question 3.7

Note: You should use the email address actively used by the respondent for personal emails. Where the respondent has a solicitor who is instructed to accept service of the application, please insert the solicitor's email address here instead.

The email address should not be the same as the one given for the sole applicant/ applicant 1.

Page 7

3.4 Is the application to be served on the respondent outside England and Wales?

☐ Yes. You must arrange service of this application on the respondent. **Go to question 3.6.**

☐ No

Note 3.4: If the respondent to a sole application is not in England and Wales the applicant must arrange to serve this application on the respondent. Special rules about service may apply and you may wish to seek legal advice.

3.5 The court will serve the application on the respondent by email and a notice sent by post unless you tick the box below

☐ Please serve this application by post only

☐ I will arrange service on the respondent

3.6 Has the respondent provided a different address for the court documents to be sent to?

☐ Yes, please complete the address details below

☐ No. **Go to Section 4.**

Note 3.6: Alternative addresses or solicitor addresses should be provided at question 3.10.

3.7 The solicitor's name for the respondent or applicant 2 (if applicable and if known)

3.8 The solicitor's reference number (if applicable and if known)

3.9 Name of the solicitor's firm (if applicable and if known)

3.10 The solicitor's or other address they have provided

Building and street

Second line of address

Town or city

County (optional)

Country

Postcode

DX address (if applicable)

Phone number

Note 3.10: The court will send documents to this address.

Page 9

Section 4 – Details of marriage/civil partnership

Note: If you are applying without your marriage/civil partnership certificate you will need to make a separate application on form **D11** (Application notice) and pay another court fee. It is recommended that you seek legal advice if you are unsure of how to do this.

You should attach your marriage or civil partnership certificate to this application, together with a certified translation in English if necessary (the court will usually keep your documents and not return them). If you do not have the original certificate and cannot get a copy of it, you will have to make a separate application, alongside this application, to issue this form without it.

4.1 Did your marriage/civil partnership take place outside of the UK?

☐ Yes

☐ No

4.2 Are you making a separate application to issue without your marriage or civil partnership certificate?

☐ Yes

☐ No

If you answered 'Yes', to either question 4.1 or 4.2 above, please give the place where the marriage/civil partnership was formed, as it appears on your marriage/civil partnership certificate (if any)

4.3 Date of marriage or civil partnership

Note 4.3: You can only apply for a divorce/dissolution if you have been in your marriage or civil partnership for at least one year.

Day

Month

Year

4.4 Your full name as shown on your certificate

Your spouse/civil partner's full name as shown on your certificate

4.5 Are the details set out in your marriage or civil partnership certificate correct?

☐ Yes

☐ No. Please explain why

Section 5 – Why this court can deal with your case (Jurisdiction)

The court needs to understand why you think it has the legal power (jurisdiction) to deal with your application.

Please complete section 5.1 or if that section does not apply to you then complete section 5.2.

Important: If you need help deciding which reasons apply to you then you should consider seeking legal advice, particularly if you live outside England and Wales.

5.1 The usual basis for the court to have jurisdiction is where one or both parties are habitually resident in England and Wales.

Habitual Residence

Your habitual residence is the place in which your life is mainly based. You must be settled there and intend to stay settled there. Some of the following may apply: you work there, own property, have your children in school there, and your main family life takes place there.

Domicile

Your domicile is the place of your permanent home in which you live, or to which you intend to return.

When you were born you will have acquired your parents' domicile (for example, your father's if they were married, or your mother's if they weren't married or if your father died before you were born). If you have since moved to another country and made that your permanent home then your domicile may have moved there.

If you were born in England or Wales, lived your entire life here, and intend to stay here, then it is very likely that you'll be **both habitually resident and domiciled** here.

As the court will need to know the reason(s) for why you think it has jurisdiction to deal with the application, please tick the reason(s) from the list over the page.

Please tick the reasons that apply:

- ☐ both parties to the marriage/civil partners are habitually resident in England and Wales;
- ☐ both parties to the marriage/civil partners were last habitually resident in England and Wales and one of them continues to reside there;
- ☐ the respondent is habitually resident in England and Wales;
- ☐ this is a joint application and either
  - ☐ applicant 1

  or
  - ☐ applicant 2

  is habitually resident in England and Wales;
- ☐ the applicant is habitually resident in England and Wales and has resided there for at least one year immediately before the application was made;
- ☐ the applicant is domiciled and habitually resident in England and Wales and has resided there for at least six months immediately before the application was made;
- ☐ both parties to the marriage/civil partners are domiciled in England and Wales; **or**
- ☐ only
  - ☐ applicant/applicant 1
  - ☐ applicant 2
  - ☐ respondent

  is domiciled in England and Wales.

OR for civil partners or same sex marriage only

5.2 If the options in section 5.1 do not apply to you, please consider if below is applicable:

- ☐ the parties registered as civil partners of each other in England or Wales or, in the case of a same sex couple, married each other under the law of England and Wales and it would be in the interests of justice for the court to assume jurisdiction in this case.

Page 13

Section 6 – Statement of irretrievable breakdown (the legal reason for your divorce or dissolution)

6.1 You must state that your marriage or civil partnership has broken down irretrievably in order for the court to make an order.

If a joint application applicant 1 and applicant 2 must each make a statement by ticking the box that applies to them.

Sole applicant or applicant 1

☐ I confirm that my marriage or civil partnership has broken down irretrievably

Applicant 2 (if a joint application)

☐ I confirm that my marriage or civil partnership has broken down irretrievably

Section 7 – Existing or previous court cases

7.1 Are there any existing or previous court proceedings relating to your marriage/civil partnership or affecting its validity (including any existing or concluded court proceedings overseas)?

☐ Yes, please give details below

☐ No

Case number(s)

Summary of the existing or previous court proceedings

Note 7: Joint applicants are to complete the details necessary together in the same box provided.

Section 8 – Dividing your money and property – Orders which are sought

You can apply to the court about how your money, property, pensions and other assests are to be split. These are called financial orders and may include

- an order for maintenance pending suit/outcome
- periodical payments order
- secured provision order
- lump sum order
- property adjustment order
- Pension sharing/compensation sharing/attachment order

You can apply for orders for yourself, and/or, if appropriate for your children.

If you agree with your spouse or civil partner about how your property, money, pensions and other assets will be split, and want it to be legally binding, you can apply for a financial order to be made by consent.

If you disagree with your spouse or civil partner about how your property, money, pensions and other assets will be split, then you can ask the court to decide for you.

8.1 Do you want to apply for a financial order?

Sole applicant or applicant 1

☐ Yes, I want to apply for a financial order for (select all that apply)

☐ myself

☐ the children

☐ No

Applicant 2

☐ Yes, I want to apply for a financial order for (select all that apply)

☐ myself

☐ the children

☐ No

Money and property when you divorce or separate
You may be able to solve your financial and other arrangements outside of court, for example through mediation. You can find more information on mediation at https://www.gov.uk/money-property-when-relationship-ends/mediation

If you answer 'Yes' to question 8.1 the court will take no action at this stage. To formally start financial proceedings, you will also need to complete a separate application **Form A** or **Form A1** and pay another court fee.

You can find more guidance on financial orders and how to get help agreeing on any issues at www.gov.uk/money-property-when-relationship-ends/apply-for-a-financial-order

If you answer 'No' to question 8.1 you can still apply for a financial order in the future, but only **until you remarry or form** another **civil partnership**. This restriction does not apply to pension sharing or pension compensation sharing orders.

If you are unsure what to do here it is recommended you seek legal advice.

Please note that decisions regarding child maintenance are usually made by agreement or by the Child Maintenance Service and the court can only make these orders under certain circumstances.

Page 15

Section 9 – Summary of what is being applied for (the prayer)

The sole applicant or the joint applicants apply for the following:

9.1 The application

That the

☐ marriage be dissolved

☐ civil partnership be dissolved

The sole applicant or applicant 1 wishes to apply for the following

9.2 Financial Order (if you ticked 'Yes' to the question at 8.1 and wish to make an application for a Financial Order)

That a financial order may be granted for:

☐ The sole applicant or applicant 1

☐ For the children

Applicant 2 wishes to apply for the following

9.3 Financial Order (if you ticked 'Yes' to the question at 8.1 and wish to make an application for a Financial Order)

That a financial order may be granted for:

☐ Applicant 2

☐ For the children

Section 10 – Statement of truth

10.1 Sole applicant or applicant 1

I understand that proceedings for contempt of court may be brought against anyone who makes, or causes to be made, a false statement in a document verified by a statement of truth without an honest belief in its truth.

☐ **I believe** that the facts stated in this form and any continuation sheets are true.

☐ **The applicant** believes that the facts stated in this form and any continuation sheets are true. **I am authorised** by the applicant to sign this statement.

Signature

☐ Applicant

☐ Applicant's legal representative (as defined by FPR 2.3(1))

Date

Day Month Year

Full name

Name of applicant's legal representative's firm

If signing on behalf of firm or company give position or office held

10.2 Applicant 2

I understand that proceedings for contempt of court may be brought against anyone who makes, or causes to be made, a false statement in a document verified by a statement of truth without an honest belief in its truth.

☐ **I believe** that the facts stated in this form and any continuation sheets are true.

☐ **The applicant** believes that the facts stated in this form and any continuation sheets are true. **I am authorised** by the applicant to sign this statement.

Signature

☐ Applicant

☐ Applicant's legal representative (as defined by FPR 2.3(1))

Date

Day Month Year

Full name

Name of applicant's legal representative's firm

If signing on behalf of firm or company give position or office held

Court fee

What you need to pay

the court fee is

How to pay the court fee

Sole or applicant 1

☐ **I have not included payment because**

☐ I have applied for Help with Fees online and my reference number is

H	W	F						

☐ I am applying for Help with Fees, see attached form **EX160**

☐ Other – please explain why

Applicant 2

☐ **I have not included payment because**

☐ I have applied for Help with Fees online and my reference number is

H	W	F						

☐ I am applying for Help with Fees, see attached form **EX160**

☐ Other – please explain why

☐ **A debit or credit card payment**

☐ I will pay over the phone.

☐ please email me details on how to pay, my email address is

☐ I attach a **cheque or postal order,** made payable to 'HMCTS'

Court fee
You can find the current fee in leaflet EX50 Civil and Family Court Fees which can be downloaded from: https://hmctsformfinder.justice.gov.uk

If you cannot afford the court fee

You may not have to pay a fee, or you may get some money off it if you only have a small amount of savings and investments, receive certain benefits or are on a low income.

You can apply for help with court and tribunal fees online at www.gov.uk/help-with-court-fees or through the 'EX160 Apply for help with fees' form and 'EX160A – How to apply for help with fees' guidance.

If applying jointly, both applicant 1 and applicant 2 must qualify for HWF, or the full fee will be payable by one applicant only. You can decide how you wish to share the cost of the fee. Then you must agree who will make the payment to the court.

A debit or credit card payment. To pay the court fee over the phone, you should call the payment line **10 days after** you submit the application to court on 0300 303 0642 (Monday to Friday: 8am to 6pm, Saturday 8am to 2pm)

When returning your form, you must include:

- **One original or certified** copy of your marriage/civil partnership certificate or a similar document issued under the law in force in the country where the marriage or civil partnership registration took place (photocopies will not be accepted). If your certificate is not in English then a certified translation must also be provided. The court will keep the documents you send. If you want them back you will need to apply for their return.
- **The court fee**
  You can find the current fee in leaflet **EX50** Civil and Family Court Fees which can be downloaded from: https://www.gov.uk/government/collections/court-and-tribunal-forms

  If you cannot afford to pay a court fee, you may be eligible for a fee remission or a reduced fee. The form **EX160** Apply for help with fees and the **EX160A** guidance booklet gives you further information – https://www.gov.uk/get-help-with-court-fees

Please send your application and the items listed above to

HMCTS Divorce and Dissolution service
PO Box 13226
Harlow
CM20 9UG

Phone: 0300 303 0642
Monday to Friday: 8am to 6pm
Saturday 8am to 2pm

email: divorcecase@justice.gov.uk

Cheque payments only

If you are paying by cheque, remember to include it with your application and make it payable to 'HMCTS'.

You must send your completed application and cheque to:

Bury St Edmunds Regional Divorce Unit
Triton House
St Andrew's Street North
Bury St Edmunds
IP33 1TR

APPENDIX TWO

FAMILY PROCEDURE RULES, PART 6

From:
https://www.justice.gov.uk/courts/procedure-rules/family/parts/part_06

PART 6 – SERVICE

This Part applies to applications issued by the court on or after 6 April 2022.

. . .

I SCOPE OF THIS PART AND INTERPRETATION

Part 6 rules about service apply generally

6.1

This Part applies to the service of documents, except where –

(a) another Part, any other enactment or a practice direction makes a different provision; or

(b) the court directs otherwise.**Interpretation**

6.2

In this Part 'solicitor' includes any person who, for the purposes of the Legal Services Act 2007, is an authorised person in relation to an activity which constitutes the conduct of litigation (within the meaning of that Act).

II SERVICE OF THE APPLICATION FOR A MATRIMONIAL ORDER OR CIVIL PARTNERSHIP ORDER IN THE JURISDICTION

Interpretation

6.3

In this Chapter, unless the context otherwise requires, a reference to an application –

(a) is a reference to an application for a matrimonial or civil partnership order; and

(b) includes an application by a respondent.

('Jurisdiction' is defined in rule 2.3.)

(Part 7 deals with applications in matrimonial or civil partnership proceedings.)

Methods of service

6.4

An application may be served by any of the following methods –

(a) personal service in accordance with rule 6.7;

(b) first class post, or other service which provides for delivery on the next business day, in accordance with Practice Direction 6A;

(c) where rule 6.11 applies, document exchange; or

(d) email service in accordance with rule 6.7A.

Who is to serve the application

6.5

(1) Subject to the provisions of this rule, an application may be served by –

(a) a court officer; or

(b) the applicant, if so requested by the applicant.

(2) A court officer will not serve the application if the party to be served is—

(a) a child or protected party; or

(b) out of the jurisdiction.

(3) An application must not be served personally by the applicant himself or herself.

(Rule 6.14 deals with service of the application on children and protected parties.)

The respondent to be served

6.6

The application must be served on every respondent.

Time for serving an application by the applicant

6.6A

Where the applicant serves the application, the applicant must complete the step required by the following table in relation to the method of service chosen before 12.00 midnight on the day 28 days after the date of issue of the application.

Method of service	Step required
First class post, document exchange or other service which provides for delivery on the next business day	Posting, leaving with, delivering to or collection by the relevant service provider
Personal service under rule 6.7, by someone other than the applicant personally	Leaving it with the person to be served
Email service under rule 6.7A	Sending the application by e-mail and sending the notice required by rule 6.7A(2) by posting, leaving with, delivering to or collection by the relevant service provider

Extension of time for serving the application

6.6B

(1) The applicant may apply for an order extending the time for compliance with rule 6.6A.

(2) The general rule is that an application under paragraph (1) must be made—

(a) within the period for service specified by rule 6.6A; or

(b) where an order has been made under this rule, within the period specified by that order.

(3) Where an applicant asserts that they have a good reason for not making an application under paragraph (1) within a period specified in paragraph (2) an application under paragraph (1) may be made—

(a) after the period for service specified by rule 6.6A; or

(b) where an order has been made under this rule, after the period specified by that order.

(4) On an application under paragraph (1), the court must consider all the circumstances including whether—

(a) the court has failed to serve the application;

(b) the applicant has taken reasonable steps to comply with rule 6.6A; and

(c) the applicant has acted promptly.

(5) An application for an order extending the time for compliance with rule 6.6A—

(a) must be supported by evidence; and

(b) may be made without notice.

(6) Where an order is made without notice—

(a) a copy of the order; and

(b) a copy of the application for an order extending time together with any statement supporting it, must be served on the respondent when the application for a matrimonial or civil partnership order is served.

Personal service

6.7

An application is served personally on a respondent by leaving it with that respondent.

Email service

6.7A

(1) Subject to paragraph (2), an application is served on a respondent by email by sending it to—

(a)the respondent's usual email address; or

(b) the email address provided by the respondent in accordance with rule 6.12.

(2) Where an application is served by email, a notice confirming such service must be sent to the respondent's postal address, by first class post or other service which provides for delivery on the next business day

Service of application by the court

6.8

(1) Where the application is to be served by a court officer, the applicant must give the court officer—

(a) the respondent's usual email address (if known); and

(b) the respondent's last known or usual postal address,

at which the respondent is to be served in accordance with rule 6.4.

(2) Subject to paragraph (3), a court officer will serve the application by email in accordance with rule 6.7A.

(3) Where—

(a) an email address for service on the respondent is not provided; or

(b) the applicant does not seek email service on the respondent,

a court officer will serve the application by first class post or other service which provides for delivery on the next business day.

(4) Where the court officer has sent to the applicant a notification of failure of service in accordance with rule 6.21 (postal service) or 6.21A (email service), the applicant may request the court officer to serve the document on the respondent at an alternative address.

(5) Where the court officer has served the respondent following a request in accordance with paragraph (4), the court will not try to serve the application again.

Service by the bailiff

6.9

(1) An applicant may request that an application be served by a bailiff delivering a copy of the application to the respondent personally.

(2) The request must be made in accordance with Practice Direction 6A.

(3) Where the bailiff is unable to serve the application, the applicant may apply to the court for an order under rule 6.19 (service by an alternative method or at an alternative place).

(Practice Direction 6A contains provision about when a request under this rule is appropriate.)

(Rule 6.22 provides for notice of non-service by a bailiff.)

Where to serve the application – general provisions

6.10

(1) The application must be served within the jurisdiction except as provided for by Chapter 4 of this Part (service out of the jurisdiction).

(2) The applicant must include in the application—

(a) an email address (if this is known); and

(b) a postal address,

at which the respondent may be served.

(3) Paragraph (2) does not apply where an order made by the court under rule 6.19 (service by an alternative method or at an alternative place) specifies the place or method of service of the application.

Service of the application on a solicitor within the jurisdiction

6.11

(1) Where a solicitor acting for the respondent has notified the applicant in writing that the solicitor is instructed by the respondent to accept service of the application on behalf of the respondent at a

business address within the jurisdiction, the application must be served at the business address of that solicitor.

'Solicitor' has the extended meaning set out in rule 6.2)

Service of the application where the respondent gives an email address in accordance with rule 6.7A or at a postal address at which the respondent may be served

6.12

Subject to rule 6.13, the respondent may be served with the application at an address within the jurisdiction which the respondent has given for the purpose of being served with the proceedings.

Service of the application where the respondent does not give an address at which the respondent may be served

6.13

(1) This rule applies where –

(a) rule 6.11 (service of application on solicitor); and

(b) rule 6.12 (respondent gives address at which respondent may be served),

do not apply and the applicant does not wish the application to be served personally under rule 6.7.

(2) Subject to paragraphs (3) to (5) the application must be served on the respondent—

(a) if the respondent's usual email address is known, at that address in accordance with rule 6.7A; or

(b) if that usual email address is not known, or if the applicant does not seek email service on the respondent, at the respondent's usual or last known postal address.

(3) Where the applicant has reason to believe that the respondent no longer resides at his usual or last known postal address or no longer has access to the usual email address, the applicant must take reasonable steps to ascertain the current postal and email address of the respondent.

(4) Where, having taken the reasonable steps required by paragraph (3), the applicant –

(a) ascertains the respondent's current postal and email address, the application must be served in accordance with paragraph (2); or

(b) is unable to ascertain the respondent's current postal and email address, the applicant must consider whether there is –

(i) an alternative place where; or

(ii) an alternative method by which,

service may be effected.

(5) If, under paragraph (4)(b), there is such a place where or a method by which service could be effected, the applicant must make an application under rule 6.19.

Service of the application on children and protected parties

6.14

(1) Where the respondent is a child, the application form must be served on –

(a) one of the child's parents or guardians; or

(b) if there is no parent or guardian, an adult with whom the child resides or in whose care the child is.

(2) Where the respondent is a protected party, the application must be served on –

(a) one of the following persons with authority in relation to the protected party –

(i) the attorney under a registered enduring power of attorney;

(ii) the donee of a lasting power of attorney; or

(iii) the deputy appointed by the Court of Protection; or

(b) if there is no such person, an adult with whom the protected party resides or in whose care the protected party is.

(3) Any reference in this Chapter to a respondent or party to be served includes the person to be served with the application form on behalf of a child or protected party under paragraph (1) or (2).

(4) The court may make an order permitting an application form to be served on a child or protected party, or on a person other than the person specified in paragraph (1) or (2).

(5) An application for an order under paragraph (4) may be made without notice.

(6) The court may order that, although an application form has been sent or given to someone other than the person specified in paragraph (1) or (2), it is to be treated as if it had been properly served.

(7) Where a document is served in accordance with this rule –

(a) it must be endorsed with the notice set out in Practice Direction 6A; and

(b) the person commencing the proceedings must file a witness statement by the person on whom the application form was served stating whether –

(i) the contents of the application form; or

(ii) the purpose and intention of the application,

were communicated to the child or protected party and, if not, why not.

(8) Paragraph (7)(b) does not apply where the Official Solicitor is, as the case may be –

(a) the litigation friend of the protected party; or

(b) the litigation friend or children's guardian of the child.

Deemed service – receipt of acknowledgment of service

6.15

(1) Subject to paragraph (2), an application is deemed to be served if the acknowledgment of service, signed by the party served or the solicitor acting on that party's behalf, is returned to the court office.

(2) Where the signature on the acknowledgment of service purports to be that of the other party to the marriage or civil partnership, the applicant must prove that it is the signature of that party by –

(a) giving oral evidence to that effect at the hearing; or

(b) if the application is not disputed, confirming it to be so in the statement the applicant files under rule 7.9(4).

Deemed service by post or alternative service where no acknowledgment of service filed

6.16

(1) Subject to paragraph (2), if –

(a) an application has been served on a respondent by email in accordance with rule 6.7A or by post or other service which provides for delivery on the next business day;

(b) no acknowledgment of service has been returned to the court office; and

(c) the court is satisfied that the respondent has received the application,

the court may direct that the application is deemed to be served.

Proof of personal service where no acknowledgment of service filed

6.17

(1) This rule applies where –

(a) an application has been served on a respondent personally; and

(b) no acknowledgment of service has been returned to the court office.

(2) The person serving the application must file a certificate of service stating the date and time of personal service.

(Practice Direction 6A makes provision for a certificate of service by a bailiff.)

(3) If the respondent served was the other party to the marriage or civil partnership, the certificate of service must show the means by which the person serving the application knows the identity of the party served.

Proof of service by the court etc.

6.18

(1) Where a court officer serves an application by post, or other service which provides for delivery on the next business day, the court officer must note in the court records the date of –

(a) posting; or

(b) leaving with, delivering to or collection by the relevant service provider.

(2) A record made in accordance with paragraph (1) is evidence of the facts stated in it.

(3) This rule does not affect the operation of section 31N of the 1984 Act[3].

(Section 31N of the 1984 Act provides that where a summons or other process issued from the family court is served by an officer of a court, service may be proved by a certificate in a prescribed form.)

(1A) Where a court officer serves an application by email in accordance with rule 6.7A, the court officer must note in the court records the date and time of the email and the date on which the accompanying notice was posted.

Service of the application by an alternative method or at an alternative place

6.19

(1) Where it appears to the court that there is a good reason to authorise service by a method or at a place not otherwise permitted by this Part, the court may direct that service is effected by an alternative method or at an alternative place.

(2) On an application under this rule, the court may direct that steps already taken to bring the application form to the attention of the respondent by an alternative method or at an alternative place is good service.

(3) A direction under this rule must specify –

(a) the method or place of service;

(b) the date on which the application form is deemed served; and

(c) the period for filing an acknowledgment of service or answer.

Power of the court to dispense with service of the application

6.20

(1) The court may dispense with service of the application where it is impracticable to serve the application by any method provided for by this Part.

(2) An application for an order to dispense with service may be made at any time and must be supported by evidence.

(3) The court may require the applicant to attend when it decides the application.

Notification of failure postal service by the court

6.21

Where –

(a) the court serves the application by post or other service which provides for delivery on the next business day; and

(b) the application is returned to the court,

the court will send notification to the applicant that the application has been returned.

Notification of failure of email service by the court

6.21A

Where –

(a) the court officer serves the application by email in accordance with rule 6.7A; and

(b) the court is notified that the email was undeliverable,

the court officer will send notification to the applicant that the application was undeliverable.

Notice of non-service by bailiff

6.22

Where –

(a) the bailiff is to serve an application; and

(b) the bailiff is unable to serve it on the respondent,

the court officer will send notification to the applicant.

III SERVICE OF DOCUMENTS OTHER THAN AN APPLICATION FOR A MATRIMONIAL ORDER OR CIVIL PARTNERSHIP ORDER IN THE UNITED KINGDOM

Method of service

6.23

A document may be served by any of the following methods –

(a) personal service, in accordance with rule 6.25;

(b) first class post, document exchange or other service which provides for delivery on the next business day, in accordance with Practice Direction 6A;

(c) leaving it at a place specified in rule 6.26; or

(d) fax or e-mail in accordance with Practice Direction 6A.

(Rule 6.35 provides for the court to permit service by an alternative method or at an alternative place.)

Who is to serve

6.24

(1) A party to proceedings will serve a document which that party has prepared, or which the court has prepared or issued on behalf of that party, except where –

(a) a rule or practice direction provides that the court will serve the document; or

(b) the court directs otherwise.

(2) Where a court officer is to serve a document, it is for the court to decide which method of service is to be used.

(3) Where the court officer is to serve a document prepared by a party, that party must provide a copy for the court and for each party to be served.

https://www.justice.gov.uk/courts/procedure-rules/family/parts/part_06 - pagetop**Personal service**

6.25

(1) Where required by another Part, any other enactment, a practice direction or a court order, a document must be served personally.

(2) In other cases, a document may be served personally except where the party to be served has given an address for service under rule 6.26(2)(a).

(3) A document is served personally on an individual by leaving it with that individual.

Address for service

6.26

(1) A party to proceedings must give an address at which that party may be served with documents relating to those proceedings.

(2) Subject to paragraph (4), a party's address for service must be –

(a) the business address within the United Kingdom of a solicitor acting for the party to be served; or

(b) where there is no solicitor acting for the party to be served, an address within the United Kingdom at which the party resides or carries on business.

(3) Where there is no solicitor acting for the party to be served and the party does not have an address within the United Kingdom at which that party resides or carries on business, the party must, subject to paragraph (4), give an address for service within the United Kingdom.

(4) A party who –

(a) has been served with an application for a matrimonial or civil partnership order outside the United Kingdom; and

(b) apart from acknowledging service of the application, does not take part in the proceedings,

need not give an address for service within the United Kingdom.

(5) Any document to be served in proceedings must be sent, or transmitted to, or left at, the party's address for service unless it is to be served personally or the court orders otherwise.

(6) Where, in accordance with Practice Direction 6A, a party indicates or is deemed to have indicated that they will accept service by fax, the fax number given by that party must be at the address for service.

(7) Where a party indicates in accordance with Practice Direction 6A, that they will accept service by e-mail, the e-mail address given by that party will be deemed to be the address for service.

(8) This rule does not apply where an order made by the court under rule 6.35 (service by an alternative method or at an alternative place) specifies where a document may be served.

Change of address for service

6.27

Where the address for service of a party changes, that party must give notice in writing of the change, as soon as it has taken place, to the court and every other party.

Service of an application form commencing proceedings on children and protected parties

6.28

(1) This rule applies to the service of an application form commencing proceedings other than an application for a matrimonial or civil partnership order.

(2) An application form commencing proceedings which would otherwise be served on a child or protected party must be served –

(a) where the respondent is a child, in accordance with rule 6.14(1); and

(b) where the respondent is a protected party, in accordance with rule 6.14(2).

Service of other documents on or by children and protected parties where a litigation friend has been or will be appointed

6.29

(1) This rule applies to –

(a) a protected party; or

(b) a child to whom the provisions of rule 16.5 and Chapter 5 of Part 16 apply (litigation friends).

(2) An application for an order appointing a litigation friend where a protected party or child has no litigation friend must be served in accordance with rule 15.8 or rule 16.13 as the case may be.

(3) Any other document which would otherwise be served on or by a child or protected party must be served on or by the litigation friend conducting the proceedings on behalf of the child or protected party.

Service on or by children where a children's guardian has been or will be appointed under rule 16.4

6.30

(1) This rule applies to a child to whom the provisions of rule 16.4 and Chapter 7 apply.

(2) An application for an order appointing a children's guardian where a child has no children's guardian must be served in accordance with rule 16.26.

(3) Any other document which would otherwise be served on or by a child must be served on or by the children's guardian conducting the proceedings on behalf of the child.

Service on or by children where a children's guardian has been appointed under rule 16.3

6.31

(1) This rule applies where a children's guardian has been appointed for a child in accordance with rule 16.3.

(2) Any document which would otherwise be served on the child must be served on –

(a) the solicitor appointed by the court in accordance with section 41(3) of the 1989 Act; and

(b) the children's guardian.

(3) Any document which would otherwise be served by the child must be served by –

(a) the solicitor appointed by the court in accordance with section 41(3) of the 1989 Act or by the children's guardian; or

(b) if no solicitor has been appointed as mentioned in paragraph (a), the children's guardian.

Supplementary provisions relating to service on children and protected parties

6.32

(1) The court may direct that a document be served on a protected party or child or on some person other than a person upon whom it would be served under rules 6.28 to 6.31 above.

(2) The court may direct that, although a document has been sent or given to someone other than a person upon whom it should be served under rules 6.28 to 6.31 above, the document is to be treated as if it had been properly served.

(3) This rule and rules 6.28 to 6.31 do not apply where the court has made an order under rule 16.6 allowing a child to conduct proceedings without a children's guardian or litigation friend.

Supplementary provision relating to service on children

6.33

(1) This rule applies to proceedings to which Part 12 applies.

(2) Where a rule requires –

(a) a document to be served on a party;

(b) a party to be notified of any matter; or

(c) a party to be supplied with a copy of a document,

in addition to the persons to be served in accordance with rules 6.28 to 6.32, the persons or bodies mentioned in paragraph (3) must be served, notified or supplied with a copy of a document, as applicable, unless the court directs otherwise.

(3) The persons or bodies referred to in paragraph (2) are –

(a) such of the following who are appointed in the proceedings-

(i) the children's guardian (if the children's guardian is not otherwise to be served);

(ii) the welfare officer;

(iii) the children and family reporter;

(iv) the officer of the Service, Welsh family proceedings officer or local authority officer acting under a duty referred to in rule 16.38; and

(b) a local authority preparing a report under section 14A(8) or (9) of the 1989 Act.

Deemed service

6.34

A document, other than an application for a matrimonial or civil partnership order, served in accordance with these rules or a practice direction is deemed to be served on the day shown in the following table –

Method of service	Deemed day of service
First class post (or other service which provides for delivery on the next business day)	The second day after it was posted, left with, delivered to or collected by the relevant service provider, provided that day is a business day; or, if not, the next business day after that day
Document exchange	The second day after it was left with, delivered to or collected by the relevant service provider, provided that day is a business day; or, if not, the next business day after that day
Delivering the document to or leaving it at a permitted address	If it is delivered to or left at the permitted address on a business day before 4.30p.m., on that day; or in any other case, on the next business day after that day
Fax.	If the transmission of the fax is completed on a business day before 4.30p.m., on that day; or, in any other case, the next

Method of service	Deemed day of service
	business day after the day on which it was transmitted
Other electronic method	If the e-mail or other electronic transmission is sent on a business day before 4.30p.m., on that day; or in any other case, on the next business day after the day on which it was sent
Personal service	If the document is served personally before 4.30p.m. on a business day, on that day; or, in any other case, on the next business day after that day

(Practice Direction 6A contains examples of how the date of deemed service is calculated.)

Service by an alternative method or at an alternative place

6.35

Rule 6.19 applies to any document in proceedings as it applies to an application for a matrimonial or civil partnership order and reference to the respondent in that rule is modified accordingly.

Power to dispense with service

6.36

The court may dispense with the service of any document which is to be served in proceedings.

Certificate of service

6.37

(1) Where a rule, practice direction or court order requires a certificate of service, the certificate must state the details set out in the following table –

Method of service	Details to be certified
Personal service	Date and time of personal service and method of identifying the person served
First class post, document exchange or other service which provides for delivery on the next business day	Date of posting, leaving with, delivering to or collection by the relevant service provider
Delivery of document to or leaving it at a permitted place	Date and time when the document was delivered to or left at the permitted place
Fax.	Date and time of completion of transmission
Other electronic method	Date and time of sending the email or other electronic transmission

Method of service	Details to be certified
Alternative method or place permitted by court	As required by the court

(2) An applicant who is required to file a certificate of service of an application form must do so at or before the earlier of –

(a) the first directions appointment in; or

(b) the hearing of,

the proceedings unless a rule or practice direction provides otherwise.

(Rule 17.2 requires a certificate of service to contain a statement of truth.)

Notification of outcome of service by the court

6.38

Where –

(a) a document to be served by a court officer is served by post or other service which provides for delivery on the next working day; and

(b) the document is returned to the court,

the court officer will send notification to the party who requested service that the document has been returned.

Notification of non-service by bailiff

6.39

Where –

(a) the bailiff is to serve a document; and

(b) the bailiff is unable to serve it,

the court officer must send notification to the party who requested service.

IV SERVICE OUT OF THE JURISDICTION

Scope and interpretation

6.40

(1) This Chapter contains rules about –

(a) service of application forms and other documents out of the jurisdiction; and

(b) the procedure for service.

('Jurisdiction' is defined in rule 2.3.)

(2) In this Chapter –

'application form' includes an application notice;

'Commonwealth State' means a State listed in Schedule 3 to the British Nationality Act 1981[4]; and 'the Hague Convention' means the Convention on the service abroad of judicial and extra-judicial documents in civil or commercial matters signed at the Hague on November 15, 1965.

Permission to serve not required

6.41

Any document to be served for the purposes of these rules may be served out of the jurisdiction without the permission of the court.

Time for serving an application for a matrimonial or civil partnership order out of the jurisdiction

6.41A

(1) The applicant must complete the step required by the table in paragraph (2) or (3), as applicable, in relation to the method of service chosen before 12.00 midnight on the day 28 days after the date of issue of the application.

(2) Where service of an application for a matrimonial or civil partnership order is to be effected on a party in Scotland or Northern Ireland—

Method of service	Step required
First class post, document exchange or other service which provides for delivery on the next business day	Posting, leaving with, delivering to or collection by the relevant service provider

Method of service	Step required
Personal service under rule 6.7, by someone other than the applicant personally	Leaving it with the person to be served
Email service under rule 6.7A	Sending the application by e-mail and sending the notice required by rule 6.7A(2) by posting, leaving with, delivering to or collection by the relevant service provider

(3) Where service of an application for a matrimonial or civil partnership order is to be effected on a respondent out of the United Kingdom—

Method of service	Step required
Where service is to be effected by a method provided for by rule 6.45	The steps required by rule 6.46(2)
Where service is to be effected by another method permitted by the law of the country in which it is to be served	Sending or delivering the application to, or leaving it with, the person to be served or taking such other such steps to effect service as are permitted by the law of the country in which it is to be served

Extension of time for serving the application for a matrimonial or civil partnership order

6.41B

(1) The applicant may apply for an order extending the time for compliance with rule 6.41A.

(2) The general rule is that an application under paragraph (1) must be made—

(a) within the period for service specified by rule 6.41A; or

(b) where an order has been made under this rule, within the period specified by that order.

(3) Where an applicant asserts that they have a good reason for not making an application under paragraph (1) within the periods specified in paragraph (2) an application under paragraph (1) may be made—

(a) after the period for service specified by rule 6.41A; or

(b) where an order has been made under this rule, after the period specified by that order.

(4) On an application under paragraph (1), the court must consider all the circumstances including whether—

(a) the applicant has taken reasonable steps to comply with rule 6.41A; and

(b) the applicant has acted promptly.

(5) An application for an order extending the time for compliance with rule 6.41A—

(a) must be supported by evidence; and

(b) may be made without notice.

Period for acknowledging service or responding to application where application is served out of the jurisdiction

6.42

(1) This rule applies where, under these rules, a party is required to file –

(a) an acknowledgment of service; or

(b) an answer to an application,

and sets out the time period for doing so where the application is served out of the jurisdiction.

(2) Where the applicant serves an application on a respondent in –

(a) Scotland or Northern Ireland; or

(b) Hague Convention country within Europe,

the period for filing an acknowledgment of service or an answer to an application is 21 days after service of the application.

(3) Where the applicant serves an application on a respondent in a Hague Convention country outside Europe, the period for filing an acknowledgment of service or an answer to an application is 31 days after service of the application.

(4) Where the applicant serves an application on a respondent in a country not referred to in paragraphs (2) and (3), the period for filing

an acknowledgment of service or an answer to an application is set out in Practice Direction 6B.

Method of service – general provisions

6.43

(1) This rule contains general provisions about the method of service of an application for a matrimonial or civil partnership order, or other document, on a party out of the jurisdiction.

Where service is to be effected on a party in Scotland or Northern Ireland

(2) Where a party serves an application form or other document on a party in Scotland or Northern Ireland, it must be served by a method permitted by Chapter 2 (and references to 'jurisdiction' in that Chapter are modified accordingly) or Chapter 3 of this Part and rule 6.26(5) applies.

Where service is to be effected on a respondent out of the United Kingdom

(3) Where the applicant wishes to serve an application form, or other document, on a respondent out of the United Kingdom, it may be served by any method –

(a) provided for by –

(i) rule 6.44 (service in accordance with the Service Regulation);

(b) permitted by the law of the country in which it is to be served.

(4) Nothing in paragraph (3) or in any court order authorises or requires any person to do anything which is contrary to the law of the

country where the application form, or other document, is to be served.

6.44 Omitted

Service through foreign governments, judicial authorities and British Consular authorities

6.45

(1) Where the applicant wishes to serve an application form, or other document, on a respondent in any country which is a party to the Hague Convention, it may be served –

(a) through the authority designated under the Hague Convention in respect of that country; or

(b) if the law of that country permits –

(i) through the judicial authorities of that country; or

(ii) through a British Consular authority in that country.

(2) Where the applicant wishes to serve an application form, or other document, on a respondent in any country which is not a party to the Hague Convention, it may be served, if the law of that country so permits –

(a) through the government of that country, where that government is willing to serve it; or

(b) through a British Consular authority in that country.

(3) Where the applicant wishes to serve an application form, or other document, in –

(a) any Commonwealth State which is not a party to the Hague Convention;

(b) the Isle of Man or the Channel Islands; or

(c) any British Overseas Territory,

the methods of service permitted by paragraphs (1)(b) and (2) are not available and the applicant or the applicant's agent must effect service on a respondent in accordance with rule 6.43 unless Practice Direction 6B provides otherwise.

(A list of British overseas territories is reproduced in Practice Direction 6B.)

Procedure where service is to be through foreign governments, judicial authorities and British Consular authorities

6.46

(1) This rule applies where the applicant wishes to serve an application form, or other document, under rule 6.45(1) or (2).

(2) Where this rule applies, the applicant must file –

(a) a request for service of the application form, or other document, by specifying one or more of the methods in rule6.45(1) or (2);

(b) a copy of the application form or other document;

(c) any other documents or copies of documents required by Practice Direction 6B; and

(d) any translation required under rule 6.47.

(3) When the applicant files the documents specified in paragraph (2), the court officer will –

(a) seal[(GL)], or otherwise authenticate with the stamp of the court, the copy of the application form or other document; and

(b) forward the documents to the Senior Master of the Queen's Bench Division.

(4) The Senior Master will send documents forwarded under this rule –

(a) where the application form, or other document, is being served through the authority designated under the Hague Convention, to that authority; or

(b) in any other case, to the Foreign and Commonwealth Office with a request that it arranges for the application form or other document to be served.

(5) An official certificate which –

(a) states that the method requested under paragraph (2)(a) has been performed and the date of such performance;

(b) states, where more than one method is requested under paragraph (2)(a), which method was used; and

(c) is made by –

(i) a British Consular authority in the country where the method requested under paragraph (2)(a) was performed;

(ii) the government or judicial authorities in that country; or

(iii) the authority designated in respect of that country under the Hague Convention,

is evidence of the facts stated in the certificate.

(6) A document purporting to be an official certificate under paragraph (5) is to be treated as such a certificate, unless it is proved not to be.

Translation of application form or other document

6.47

(1) Except where paragraphs (4) and (5) apply, every copy of the application form, or other document, filed under rule 6.45 (service through foreign governments, judicial authorities and British Consular authorities) must be accompanied by a translation of the application form or other document.

(2) The translation must be –

(a) in the official language of the country in which it is to be served; or

(b) if there is more than one official language of that country, in any official language which is appropriate to the place in the country where the application form or other document is to be served.

(3) Every translation filed under this rule must be accompanied by a statement by the person making it that it is a correct translation, and the statement must include that person's name, address and qualifications for making the translation.

(4) The applicant is not required to file a translation of the application form, or other document, filed under rule 6.45 where it is to be served in a country of which English is an official language.

(5) The applicant is not required to file a translation of the application form or other document filed under rule 6.45 where –

(a) the person on whom the document is to be served is able to read and understand English; and

(b) service of the document is to be effected directly on that person.

Undertaking to be responsible for expenses of the Foreign and Commonwealth Office

6.48

Every request for service filed under rule 6.46 (procedure where service is to be through foreign governments, judicial authorities etc.) must contain an undertaking by the person making the request –

(a) to be responsible for all expenses incurred by the Foreign and Commonwealth Office or foreign judicial authority; and

(b) to pay those expenses to the Foreign and Commonwealth Office or foreign judicial authority on being informed of the amount.

Footnotes

1. 1978 c.30. Return to footnote 1

2. Section 1(2) has been prospectively repealed by section 66(3) of and Schedule 10 to the Family Law Act 1996. Return to footnote 2

3. Section 133 of the County Courts Act 1984 (c.28) was amended by the Civil Procedure (Modification of Enactments) Order 1998 (S.I.1998/2940). Return to footnote 3

4. 1981 c.61. Return to footnote 4

MORE BOOKS BY LAW BRIEF PUBLISHING

A selection of our other titles available now:-

'A Practical Guide to Document Signing and Electronic Signatures for Conveyancers' by Lorraine Richardson
'A Practical Guide to Transgender Law' by Robin Moira White & Nicola Newbegin
'Artificial Intelligence – The Practical Legal Issues (2nd Edition)' by John Buyers
'A Practical Guide to Residential Freehold Conveyancing' by Lorraine Richardson
'A Practical Guide to Pensions on Divorce for Lawyers' by Bryan Scant
'A Practical Guide to Challenging Sham Marriage Allegations in Immigration Law' by Priya Solanki
'A Practical Guide to Legal Rights in Scotland' by Sarah-Jane Macdonald
'A Practical Guide to New Build Conveyancing' by Paul Sams & Rebecca East
'A Practical Guide to Defending Barristers in Disciplinary Cases' by Marc Beaumont
'A Practical Guide to Inherited Wealth on Divorce' by Hayley Trim
'A Practical Guide to Practice Direction 12J and Domestic Abuse in Private Law Children Proceedings' by Rebecca Cross & Malvika Jaganmohan
'A Practical Guide to Confiscation and Restraint' by Narita Bahra QC, John Carl Townsend, David Winch
'A Practical Guide to the Law of Forests in Scotland' by Philip Buchan
'A Practical Guide to Health and Medical Cases in Immigration Law' by Rebecca Chapman & Miranda Butler
'A Practical Guide to Bad Character Evidence for Criminal Practitioners by Aparna Rao
'A Practical Guide to Extradition Law post-Brexit' by Myles Grandison et al
'A Practical Guide to Hoarding and Mental Health for Housing Lawyers' by Rachel Coyle
'A Practical Guide to Psychiatric Claims in Personal Injury – 2nd Edition' by Liam Ryan
'Stephens on Contractual Indemnities' by Richard Stephens

‘A Practical Guide to the EU Succession Regulation’ by Richard Frimston

‘A Practical Guide to Solicitor and Client Costs – 2nd Edition’ by Robin Dunne

‘Constructive Dismissal – Practice Pointers and Principles’ by Benjimin Burgher

‘A Practical Guide to Religion and Belief Discrimination Claims in the Workplace’ by Kashif Ali

‘A Practical Guide to the Law of Medical Treatment Decisions’ by Ben Troke

‘Fundamental Dishonesty and QOCS in Personal Injury Proceedings: Law and Practice’ by Jake Rowley

‘A Practical Guide to the Law in Relation to School Exclusions’ by Charlotte Hadfield & Alice de Coverley

‘A Practical Guide to Divorce for the Silver Separators’ by Karin Walker

‘The Right to be Forgotten – The Law and Practical Issues’ by Melissa Stock

‘A Practical Guide to Planning Law and Rights of Way in National Parks, the Broads and AONBs’ by James Maurici QC, James Neill et al

‘A Practical Guide to Election Law’ by Tom Tabori

‘A Practical Guide to the Law in Relation to Surrogacy’ by Andrew Powell

‘A Practical Guide to Claims Arising from Fatal Accidents – 2nd Edition’ by James Patience

‘A Practical Guide to the Ownership of Employee Inventions – From Entitlement to Compensation’ by James Tumbridge & Ashley Roughton

‘A Practical Guide to Asbestos Claims’ by Jonathan Owen & Gareth McAloon

‘A Practical Guide to Stamp Duty Land Tax in England and Northern Ireland’ by Suzanne O’Hara

‘A Practical Guide to the Law of Farming Partnerships’ by Philip Whitcomb

‘Covid-19, Homeworking and the Law – The Essential Guide to Employment and GDPR Issues’ by Forbes Solicitors

‘Covid-19 and Criminal Law – The Essential Guide’ by Ramya Nagesh

‘Covid-19 and Family Law in England and Wales – The Essential Guide’ by Safda Mahmood

‘A Practical Guide to the Law of Unlawful Eviction and Harassment – 2nd Edition’ by Stephanie Lovegrove

‘Covid-19, Brexit and the Law of Commercial Leases – The Essential Guide’ by Mark Shelton

‘A Practical Guide to Costs in Personal Injury Claims – 2nd Edition’ by Matthew Hoe

'A Practical Guide to the General Data Protection Regulation (GDPR) – 2nd Edition' by Keith Markham
'Ellis on Credit Hire – Sixth Edition' by Aidan Ellis & Tim Kevan
'A Practical Guide to Working with Litigants in Person and McKenzie Friends in Family Cases' by Stuart Barlow
'Protecting Unregistered Brands: A Practical Guide to the Law of Passing Off' by Lorna Brazell
'A Practical Guide to Secondary Liability and Joint Enterprise Post-Jogee' by Joanne Cecil & James Mehigan
'A Practical Guide to the Pre-Action RTA Claims Protocol for Personal Injury Lawyers' by Antonia Ford
'A Practical Guide to Neighbour Disputes and the Law' by Alexander Walsh
'A Practical Guide to Forfeiture of Leases' by Mark Shelton
'A Practical Guide to Coercive Control for Legal Practitioners and Victims' by Rachel Horman
'A Practical Guide to Rights Over Airspace and Subsoil' by Daniel Gatty
'Tackling Disclosure in the Criminal Courts – A Practitioner's Guide' by Narita Bahra QC & Don Ramble
'A Practical Guide to the Law of Driverless Cars – Second Edition' by Alex Glassbrook, Emma Northey & Scarlett Milligan
'A Practical Guide to TOLATA Claims' by Greg Williams
'A Practical Guide to Elderly Law – 2nd Edition' by Justin Patten
'A Practical Guide to Responding to Housing Disrepair and Unfitness Claims' by Iain Wightwick
'A Practical Guide to the Construction and Rectification of Wills and Trust Instruments' by Edward Hewitt
'A Practical Guide to the Law of Bullying and Harassment in the Workplace' by Philip Hyland
'How to Be a Freelance Solicitor: A Practical Guide to the SRA-Regulated Freelance Solicitor Model' by Paul Bennett
'A Practical Guide to Prison Injury Claims' by Malcolm Johnson
'A Practical Guide to the Small Claims Track - 2nd Edition' by Dominic Bright
'A Practical Guide to Advising Clients at the Police Station' by Colin Stephen McKeown-Beaumont
'A Practical Guide to Antisocial Behaviour Injunctions' by Iain Wightwick

‘Practical Mediation: A Guide for Mediators, Advocates, Advisers, Lawyers, and Students in Civil, Commercial, Business, Property, Workplace, and Employment Cases’ by Jonathan Dingle with John Sephton
‘The Mini-Pupillage Workbook’ by David Boyle
‘A Practical Guide to Crofting Law’ by Brian Inkster
‘A Practical Guide to Spousal Maintenance’ by Liz Cowell
‘A Practical Guide to the Law of Domain Names and Cybersquatting’ by Andrew Clemson
‘A Practical Guide to the Law of Gender Pay Gap Reporting’ by Harini Iyengar
‘A Practical Guide to the Rights of Grandparents in Children Proceedings’ by Stuart Barlow
‘NHS Whistleblowing and the Law’ by Joseph England
‘Employment Law and the Gig Economy’ by Nigel Mackay & Annie Powell
‘A Practical Guide to Noise Induced Hearing Loss (NIHL) Claims’ by Andrew Mckie, Ian Skeate, Gareth McAloon
‘An Introduction to Beauty Negligence Claims – A Practical Guide for the Personal Injury Practitioner’ by Greg Almond
‘Intercompany Agreements for Transfer Pricing Compliance’ by Paul Sutton
‘Zen and the Art of Mediation’ by Martin Plowman
‘A Practical Guide to the SRA Principles, Individual and Law Firm Codes of Conduct 2019 – What Every Law Firm Needs to Know’ by Paul Bennett
‘A Practical Guide to Adoption for Family Lawyers’ by Graham Pegg
‘A Practical Guide to Industrial Disease Claims’ by Andrew Mckie & Ian Skeate
‘A Practical Guide to Redundancy’ by Philip Hyland
‘A Practical Guide to Vicarious Liability’ by Mariel Irvine
‘A Practical Guide to Applications for Landlord’s Consent and Variation of Leases’ by Mark Shelton
‘A Practical Guide to Relief from Sanctions Post-Mitchell and Denton’ by Peter Causton
‘A Practical Guide to Equity Release for Advisors’ by Paul Sams
‘A Practical Guide to Financial Services Claims’ by Chris Hegarty
‘The Law of Houses in Multiple Occupation: A Practical Guide to HMO Proceedings’ by Julian Hunt
‘Occupiers, Highways and Defective Premises Claims: A Practical Guide Post-Jackson – 2nd Edition’ by Andrew Mckie

'A Practical Guide to Financial Ombudsman Service Claims' by Adam Temple & Robert Scrivenor
'A Practical Guide to Advising Schools on Employment Law' by Jonathan Holden
'A Practical Guide to Running Housing Disrepair and Cavity Wall Claims: 2nd Edition' by Andrew Mckie & Ian Skeate
'A Practical Guide to Holiday Sickness Claims – 2nd Edition' by Andrew Mckie & Ian Skeate
'Arguments and Tactics for Personal Injury and Clinical Negligence Claims' by Dorian Williams
'A Practical Guide to Drone Law' by Rufus Ballaster, Andrew Firman, Eleanor Clot
'A Practical Guide to Compliance for Personal Injury Firms Working With Claims Management Companies' by Paul Bennett
'RTA Allegations of Fraud in a Post-Jackson Era: The Handbook – 2nd Edition' by Andrew Mckie
'RTA Personal Injury Claims: A Practical Guide Post-Jackson' by Andrew Mckie
'On Experts: CPR35 for Lawyers and Experts' by David Boyle
'An Introduction to Personal Injury Law' by David Boyle

These books and more are available to order online direct from the publisher at www.lawbriefpublishing.com, where you can also read free sample chapters. For any queries, contact us on 0844 587 2383 or mail@lawbriefpublishing.com.

Our books are also usually in stock at www.amazon.co.uk with free next day delivery for Prime members, and at good legal bookshops such as Wildy & Sons.

We are regularly launching new books in our series of practical day-to-day practitioners' guides. Visit our website and join our free newsletter to be kept informed and to receive special offers, free chapters, etc.

You can also follow us on Twitter at www.twitter.com/lawbriefpub.

www.ingramcontent.com/pod-product-compliance
Lightning Source LLC
LaVergne TN
LVHW022104200926
848481LV00003B/1062